A Journey Of Riches

Dealing with Changes in Life

Table of Contents

Foreword 1

Preface 3

Chapter 1: Dealing With Changes in Life
By John Spender 5

Chapter 2: Rose-Tinted Specs
By Kay Newton 23

Chapter 3: Tattooed Business Man
By Charlie O'Shea 39

Chapter 4: Lost And Found
By Chris Drabenstott 53

Chapter 5: 'Change'
By Theera Phetmalaigul 71

Chapter 6: Living With Change
By Pavel Helstyn 87

Chapter 7: The Yin and Yang of Donald Trump: Finding Your Power in a Tsunami of Hatred
by Karen Higginbottom 111

Chapter 8: In the Now Is Love: Reconnecting in Love
By Zbigniew Tappert 127

Chapter 9: Falling Into Change
By Isabella Verzberger 143

Chapter 10: The Art Of Change
By Sharee Siva 155

About the Authors 173

Foreword

I first met John Spender when he approached me to be an interview subject for his debut feature film, *Adversity*.

Although John had never previously worked as a screen media professional, he did not allow that to impede his grand vision, and I was particularly impressed by how creatively and laterally he was able to source his production financing, how he crystalized the vision of his work's direction and purpose, and how he explored effective avenues for distribution.

The conduct and manner in which he followed through with both projects clearly spoke volumes for his passionate commitment to "walk his talk," and I would be honored to collaborate professionally with him again in the future.

Now, with his book, you can share the many true and touching, real and inspiring stories of those who have chosen to respond positively to experiences, both testing and adverse, yet ultimately enriching.

The stories featured in this book resonated deeply with me and reminded me of my own learning revelation that I experienced when recovering from a near fatal stroke:

"Life's most testing battles are ultimately won and lost in the mind;" and "Regardless of our situation, it is how we choose to respond that says everything about us—whether we like it or not!"

Ade Djajamihardja, Film & Television Producer, Author & Speaker

Preface

I created this book and chose the different experts to share their personal insights, wisdom, and experiences to assist people who may be going through challenges, adversities, or changes similar to those of the authors.

Like all of us, each author has a unique story and insight to share with you. It just may be the case that one or more of these authors have lived through an experience that is similar to your situation right now and their words are the words you need to read to help you through it. Perhaps reading about one or more of these experiences will fill in the missing piece of your puzzle, so to speak.

Storytelling has been the way humankind has communicated ideas and learning throughout our civilization. While we have become more sophisticated, and life in the modern world is more convenient, there is still much discontent and dissatisfaction with one's reality. Many people have also moved away from reading books, and they are missing out on valuable information that can help them to move forward in life with a positive outlook. I think it is important to turn off the T.V., to slow down, and to read, reflect, and take the time to appreciate everything you have in life that someone else doesn't have in their reality.

I like anthology books because they carry many different perspectives and insights on a singular topic. I find that sometimes when I'm reading a book that has just one author I gain an understanding of their perspective and writing very quickly and the reading becomes predicable. With this book and all of the books in the A Journey of Riches book series, you have many different writing styles and viewpoints that will help to shape your own perspective.

Anthology books are also great because you can start from any chapter and gain a valuable insight or a nugget of wisdom without the feeling that you have missed something from the earlier chapters.

I love reading many different types of personal development books because learning and personal growth is important to me. If you are not learning and growing, well, you're staying the same. Everything in the universe is growing, expanding, and changing. If we are not open to different ideas and different ways of thinking and being, then we can become close-minded.

The idea of this book series is to open you up to different ways of perceiving your reality, to give you hope, to give you encouragement, and to give to many avenues of thinking about the same subject. My wish for you is to feel empowered to make a decision that will best suit you in moving forward with your life. As Albert Einstein said, we cannot solve problems with the same level of thinking that created them.

With Einstein's words in mind, let your mood pick a chapter in the book and allow yourself to be guided to find the answers you seek. You may be surprised to find that the words you read are exactly what you needed to hear in your mind in order to take the next step on this amazing rollercoaster of a journey that we call life.

Chapter 1

Dealing With Changes in Life

By John Spender

There was a man at the airport sitting and waiting for his flight in the departure lounge. He heard the news that no passenger wants to hear while waiting for his flight to be called for boarding: passengers flying with xyt Airlines to xyz destination, your flight has been delayed by two hours. Two whole hours! With disappointment, he thought to himself, "I'm not going to just sit here and wait. I need a good read to lose myself in time."

After choosing a book, he walked to the counter and out of his peripheral vision he saw a box of double chocolate chip cookies, his favorite. Right in that moment two voices in his head were competing with each other. One subtle voice was saying, "You don't need those. It's processed food and it'll make you fat." The other voice was louder and seductive: "Go on. You deserve them. After all, your flight has been delayed and they are your favorite." Of course, you know which voice won. Armed with his book and double chocolate chip cookies, he casually strode towards the boarding gates and sat right in front, as the fear of missing the flight was too great to sit anywhere else.

As he sat down, the woman on the other side of the small table smiled, and he returned a smile in kind. Keen to read the new book, he began in earnest, and he reached over and took a cookie. Immediately, he found himself consuming one of the most delicious cookies he had ever tasted. As he was immersed in the book, he thought he saw the woman on the other side of the table reach over and take one of his double chocolate chip cookies, though he couldn't be certain. She was eating what looked like a cookie, but he didn't care that much as he was engrossed in such a marvelous read. Reaching over and taking another cookie he continued reading the book and enjoying the moment.

After a period of time, he definitely saw the woman next to the table take one of his cookies. He looked over at the woman and she gave a nervous smile, and he nervously smiled back and proceeded to take another cookie. Then she grabbed another cookie, and he grabbed another, and she took another one. And he took another cookie! They were going cookie-for-cookie. It was a race to see who could take the last biscuit. The woman took the last double chocolate chip cookie and broke it in half to share it with the man. He laughed and took the other half of the biscuit.

Right in that moment the flight was being called. He waved thanks to the cookie thief and made his way to the boarding gate. As he went to his seat, he was thinking about reading his book on the journey to his destination and intended to forget about the crazy woman as he laughed at the recollection. Before he sat down, he put his bag on his seat to take his book out again. But as he looked in, he couldn't believe what he saw. "Oh, no!" he thought. "If these are my cookies, then those were her cookies and she was trying to share!"

I hope you are laughing at this point. That story was inspired by Valerie Cox and her poem, "The Cookie Thief." I find it to be the perfect illustration of how we as people make assumptions about situations and how we deal with changes in life and our environment. Let me explain and break the story down to see if it rings true for you.

The truth, as I see it, is that change is in constant motion. Life is forever changing, dissolving, or evolving, and it's our resistance to change that causes problems in our lives. Using the story as an example, we see the man receiving the news that his flight is delayed which is obviously a little disappointing to hear. The quicker one can adapt to the change and accept the new situation, the more at ease one can become with the new reality of waiting longer for the anticipated flight. The choice of how you, or he, feels about that can vary and it is completely up to the mindset of the individual. Clearly, the meaning that one gives the situation determines how he feels in any given situation where the change goes against one's expectations. If the scenario isn't going to bother you in a year's time, then it's not worth one minute of your time to resist the change, especially if it is out of your control. If the situation is out of your control, then resistance is just a negative exercise in disappointment.

In the story, the man quickly found a solution to his disappointment. He bought a book to read and the not-so-healthy double chocolate chip cookies. And then he found himself in another scene of change. This brings us into present-moment awareness where the man, preoccupied with excitement about reading his new book, is taken out of the present moment. His awareness of the cookies already having been placed on the table didn't exist. He may have had the intention of taking his cookies out of the bag, but when he already saw them on the table, he assumed he already had.

How often have you misplaced your keys, wallet, or purse? For some people, it happens all the time, and so it's easy to pop out of the present moment. And some people may be afraid of the present moment through fear of the unknown. So, they distract themselves with their phones, and this gives them the feeling of safety and the familiar. Others may be addicted to being distracted by shiny objects, so to speak, and never get anything done, never having anything to show for time spent.

The present-moment reality is the truth happening in the here and now. The many other realities are perceptions of the mind based in the past or in the future. The man, from lack of awareness, believed the cookies were his and was focused on reading the book. His clouded perception created a meaning that wasn't true, and his reality changed to match his perceptions. This may seem far-fetched in this example, but how many times have you lost something and blamed it on someone else, only to discover that you yourself had misplaced the item?

I remember living in a share house in Bondi, Sydney, Australia, and I had put $1000 cash in the pocket of my jacket and had forgotten where I had placed it. I looked everywhere to no avail, and my mind began to have thoughts that perhaps one of my house mates had taken my money. Naturally, I dreaded the thought, and after becoming still and calm I remembered where I had left the cash. In the example of our story, the man arrived at his seat and found his cookies in his bag, and then the truth dawned on him. My question for you is, Where in your life are you being the cookie thief?

We have blind spots in our awareness, and, in this time in history with the technology age, we can become distracted, forgetting to completely connect with life and observe what is really happening around us. Life will give us hints and, if we ignore the signs, life will cause a little bit of havoc to get our attention. At this point, it may be too late to save what we had, but it's never too late to take responsibility, learn our lesson, and to move on. If we don't learn the lesson, the same situation will repeat until we do. Unfortunately, some people never learn, and so their challenges and changes are exactly the same for their entire lives. The places and faces are different, but the root cause is the same: unresolved mental conditioning clouding their perceptions and re-creating the reality that they believe to be true.

One of the things I've been doing for a few years is meditation, and I find that it increases my awareness of my surroundings and how I'm feeling in any given moment as I deal with the changes in a typical day. Also, it helps me to have more time before reaction mode kicks in and I am able to respond in a desired manner. My meditation practice has also allowed me to tap into and listen to my intuition and trust my instincts.

This can be absolutely critical in avoiding nasty changes, and I vividly remember a particular incident that I avoided because of this awareness.

I was running my own landscaping business in the eastern suburbs of Sydney back in 2008, and late in the afternoons I would provide quotes for prospective clients. We were working in Clovelly. The boys had gone home, and I was making my way to Coogee. I parked my ute and walked to the client's front door when I heard a soft voice say, "You're going to be in a car accident if you're not careful." I immediately turned around, but no one was there. I thought that was very strange, but I proceeded to the front door and totally forgot about it.

After quoting the job, I went back home to North Bondi. It was a beautiful summer afternoon, and the sun was shining bright as I made my way up Curlewis Street. I was going to get a bottle of wine from the Beach Road Hotel before I went home, and I wanted to make a right-hand turn at the light down Glenayr Avenue. It all happened so quickly, almost like a dream was unfolding before my very eyes. The green arrow appeared for the right turn. Before I began veering to the right, there was a guy in a white van on the opposite side of the road with his left indictor on, but he was looking at a sexy woman in a bikini walking on the footpath on the other side of the road.

I noticed that the driver, distracted by the pretty woman, wasn't slowing down for the left turn. In fact, his eyes were so consumed that he not only forgot to make the turn, but he didn't slow down at all. I shocked his eyes back to the road with my horn. As he looked up, his face was ghost white and I was stationary at this point, helpless to the situation. He managed to swerve, and his van just missed my ute by the narrowest of margins, like the width of a hair. As I looked into his eyes through my side window, I could see that he was terrified, so much so that he kept going without stopping. I was thanking my lucky stars, and all of a sudden that voice I had heard made sense. I had avoided an accident that surely would have ended with a trip to the hospital for both of us. That could have been a dramatic but unnecessary life-changing moment which I would not have wanted to deal with at any point in my life.

At the time, I had been working with a Reiki master, and she was helping me to remove various emotional blocks from my past. I was also attending crystal meditations with healers trained by John of God in Brazil, and they used to call all different types of entities into the meditation. I'm really not sure where that voice came from—my higher self, a spirit guide, or maybe an angel—but whoever it was, I'm so grateful to them and that I was open enough to receive the message.

Ever since that experience, I've known that intuition is important in life and that taking the time to develop a meditation practice feeds your connection not only with yourself but also with the universe. It's necessary to allow our emotions to guide us and to flush and cleanse our emotions, especially if we are feeling confused.

When I find myself at a crossroads, I just meditate more often and focus on my breath, allowing the answers to show up. At this moment, I have been meditating twice a day for the last 106 days. I find that, by tracking and measuring what I do, it's easier to focus, to be motivated, and I really enjoy meditating at a much deeper level.

The tool I use is Insight Timer. This is an app for your smart phone. It's very easy to use, and it's like a Facebook-type community for meditation. It's amazing. It will track your meditation habits for you. This app has helped me to tap into my natural flow of intelligence and to realize that I'm the lotus flower, not the murky water.

Think about that for a moment. As a lotus flower makes its way from the muddy bottom up through the murky water to the top of the pond, it opens into a brilliant bright blossom of color. Although submerged under brown water yet to breach the surface, the lotus flower is still a flower. It doesn't rise to the top and open into a murky muddy flower just because that's where it came from.

I haven't met a single person who doesn't have a story of hardship, a personal challenge, or, on some level, an account of self-limitation. Those challenges that relate to fear, self-sabotage, negative mind chatter, and forced changes is our murky water. Like the lotus flower, we need to move towards our own light. The reminders come from people, events, and circumstances. The more we remember our true essence and acknowledge the murky water as the gift that it provides, the closer we move towards the light sharing our natural state of being.

Your natural flow of intelligence is innate. You don't have to look for it or find it. It's in you; it's in who you truly are when you are excited about your challenges, as you know you'll be better for the experience once you've moved through them. It's in the things that make you feel passion and joy, the things in which you find your natural talent. Just like a lotus flower, your flow comes from within before it opens out in the form of an expression. The opposite is to search outside yourself, further into the murky water, separating you from your natural state or your higher self.

Now that I have covered the importance of developing our own inner guidance systems to avoid unnecessary life changes, there is another area that holds people back, and that is the fear of going for opportunities, or the fear of change. In 2010, I had a goal of becoming an international trainer with the largest seminar company in the world. The requirements were lengthy. First, you need to take their training, and if you are good enough you can become an assistant trainer for two years. Then, eventually, they will let you run their trainings. I invested $21,000usd with them and travelled to three different countries only to come up short. I was naturally disappointed, but I was grateful for the opportunity and I learned so much about myself.

About four months later, another opportunity came up with a large international Neuro-Linguistic Programming (NLP) training company, and they were having tryouts in Las Vegas. I was already certified at the master level, and so I was feeling quite confident that I would be successful this time around.

I flew all the way to Vegas from Sydney for the two-week training/tryout. The chosen trainer would board a flight from Vegas to Aukland to run a three-day training. I came up short again! The woman that was chosen was very good. She had a background in television and she also spoke with so much belief in her heart. Although I was more experienced in NLP, she had more belief in herself than I did at that time. I was bummed because I had that opportunity in the palm of my hands and I let it slip out of my grasp like a slippery fish. I watched that fish pop back into the water, and it was a sinking feeling; it was the one that got away.

It was another nineteen months before an opportunity came my way again, and, before it arrived, I was ready for it. I could hear it coming. I smelled it a mile away, and though I couldn't see it I knew an amazing opportunity was on its way. There was no chance I was going to let it slip away this time. I remember sitting on the sea cliffs watching the ocean, thoughtless, feeling the expectation of the outcome on its way. It sprang to me through a Facebook message by the last seminar leader from my Vegas experience. He was starting a new company in Ubud, Bali, and he was offering me a position. There was a catch: because it was a start-up business, he wouldn't be able to pay anyone a salary.

I would have to pay for my own flight, but my living and food arrangements would be taken care of for three months. And if things worked out, I would be offered a six-month contract. They had a contract available to run trainings in Singapore with plans to run events in Malaysia and Vietnam. This gave me something to think about.

It wasn't a straight-out yes, although I had been asking the universe to send an opportunity my way. There were a few things that I needed to consider before making such a big life change and moving overseas, even if it was only for three or nine months. I already had some savings in place, and I felt excited by the opportunity, but there still was some doubt in my mind.

I decided to seek the advice of an astrologer through an online platform to put my mind at ease. The report I received confirmed that an opportunity was indeed coming my way, that it may require me to move overseas, and that it may not be a lucrative offer financially. The report was clear that, no matter what, I should take this opportunity, as it would be an enriching experience and lead to helping a lot of people from around the world. I was sold, as the main point of being a trainer was to help others to fulfill the best versions of themselves. After speaking to a few friends, I decided to say Yes!

I've discovered that change fits into five different categories: changes we consciously make; changes others make that affect us; forced changes; environmental changes; and intuitive changes. And these changes lead back to choices. Most change starts with an awareness of our reality and the choices we make. A new set of choices leads to a new discovery and adventure, and I feel that is the best mindset to take when we find ourselves at a crossroads of change.

1. Changes we consciously make:

These are the best changes to make. It means that we have made a firm decision, and when we make firm decisions we follow through with action. Even if it leads to a mistake, that is an opportunity to grow and develop, and you can course correct making adjustments along the way. It takes you out of victimhood where it feels like life is happening to us rather than for us. The worst thing we can do is nothing and sit on the fence. To consciously decide to change is empowering, and, of course, it isn't a conscious change without the key ingredient of action. It's through action that we truly see real change take place in our lives.

This is one of the reasons for developing a vision and setting goals in life, as doing so creates an end result, something to aim for—a positive expectation for reaching the desired goal. You can also research what other people have done before you, and this gives you something to model so that you can clarify how you're going to go about things.

A mistake people make is in thinking they need to have a master plan with everything already mapped out before they begin. In the most successful movie documentary ever made, grossing over three hundred and fifty million dollars in DVD sales, *The Secret,* one of the experts, Jack Canfield, shares an analogy of driving late at night with the headlights on and only being able to see five meters ahead, and then another five meters ahead. It's the same when we decide to make a conscious decision: we don't know the outcome of our choice when the decision is made; we just know the next step, and then the next step appears.

The motivating force can either be something you are moving away from or something you are moving towards. A motivation for moving away could be a toxic relationship or a job that you are dissatisfied with, and you are not sure of your next step, or maybe you do know but you don't know how to take the next step. You just know that staying where you are is not an option anymore. This type of motivation can feel like a forced change, because we can have the sense of urgency that a change needs to be made, almost like placing your hand on a hot stove, but the difference is that we have a choice to stay or not. I'll talk more about that in my definition of a forced change.

Having a motivating force where you're happy about where you are in life, with a particular job, or about living in a certain suburb, but you want more out of yourself or your business, this would be an internal motivating force. You're moving towards what you want, as it's part of a vision, an intention, or a goal. It's a natural step in your evolution, whether that be in business, your own personal growth, or in your friendships and intimate relationships. It looks like a natural step to take and, in doing so, it will keep you in the flow of what you are doing and creating.

A great example would be the vision of Richard Branson with Virgin Airlines. Naturally, he started with a small number of planes flying a small select number of popular routes, and, as he became more successful, he expanded into different regions, like Australia. Once he became successful in that market, he launched into the Pacific Islands, and so on and so forth. The next vision he has is to launch joy rides into outer space. Obviously, there is nothing wrong with his business. This is a natural form of progression and it's closely aligned with the course of nature in many ways. Like an oak seedling naturally grows into a tall tree, it doesn't second guess its nature; it follows the course of its built-in intelligence. You can be like nature and grow into a bigger version of yourself.

2. Changes others make that affect us/forced changes:

Dealing with this type of change in an empowering way requires both radical responsibility and an ability to see situations in life from a bigger perspective--much bigger than we can see with our eyes. I write about big-picture beliefs in the second book of the *A Journey of Riches* series, "The Gift in Challenge," which highlights the benefits of seeing your reality from a much larger perspective. Changes that other people make are, in large part, out of our control–especially situations like the families we were born into, the countries of our births, policy changes of governments around the world, or if our countries are at war. These are just a few examples of many that can leave people with feelings of if-only-this-hadn't-happened. From the human point of view, it can be challenging to see our lives from a bigger perspective, but doing so can allow us to move on to bigger and better experiences in life.

Let me give you an example. Just say a young girl is emotionally and physically abused by her uncle and this causes her to grow up feeling deeply insecure and never able to keep a steady boyfriend. This is the story she is living. When we take radical responsibility for the reality we live with, we are able to change the story we are living. The story can shift from "What do you expect? I was seven years of age. How else was my life going to turn out?" to "That is the very reason I decided to work on myself, and now I can help others to live life to the fullest." The only thing that changed was the personal meaning, the perspective.

Everything that happens in our lives have both negative and positive points of view. The positive in this example is, the girl is now far more compassionate to the thoughts and feelings of others and can connect and help people through difficult experiences. A real-life example is Louise Hay, the best-selling author of *'You Can Heal Your Life'* and many more books. This book has sold over 35 million copies. It's that good. In the book, Louise shares how she was repeatedly raped as a young girl by her step-father. She struggled in life for decades until her body created cervical cancer. But then she healed the disease by forgiving herself for feeling resentment towards her step-father, and she took radical responsibility for the story she was living.

In my life, I lived through emotional, physical, and sexual abuse, and I now see it as the best thing that ever happened to me. It wasn't easy, and I lived through many years of drug and alcohol abuse as a result, and it cost me many relationships and even a seven-figure business. These experiences have lead me on a journey of seeking and discovering more of my potential. I know I'm a spiritual being having a human experience. I know that we choose our parents, and I understand that we choose where we are born.

It's our responsibility to see strength in our adversities and we don't need to reinvent the wheel to change the way we see our current circumstances. Changes other people make that affect our lives can seem completely unfair in the moment. Over time, if you can step out of victimhood or the poor-me mentality and connect deeply to the beat of your own drum, the adversity becomes necessary to build your character into the person you need to be to fulfill your soul's calling. The seemingly forced change is just what you needed in order to be able to live a happy, fulfilling life and to make a difference to humanity.

3. Environmental changes:

These are the changes in the seasons. Most countries in the world have four seasons, unless you live in the tropics, and then you have two seasons: the wet season and the dry season. In the Northern Hemisphere, especially around Europe, environmental change triggers many people to commit suicide in the winter because it is so dark and cold. The rates of depression also increase as the days become shorter, the levels of light decrease, and the temperatures drop. This can also feel like forced change or changes that are out of our control.

I don't like the winter months in Australia, and that isn't considered cold by many people. I would travel in the winter months to a warmer destination and, in fact, the last time I experienced a full winter was in 2001. We're not trees. We have far greater control over where we live than a lot of people realize. A friend of mine from Brazil was living in London for a year, and he found the weather to be a difficult challenge. He found himself experiencing a period of depression while coming to terms with a long winter. I, for one, wouldn't chose to spend an entire winter in Europe, or any country for that matter, and that's one of the reasons of why I love living in Bali: the weather is warm all year round.

The most dramatic of the environmental changes is, of course, the extreme weather patterns like droughts, earthquakes, floods, hurricanes, bush fires, just to name a few. These can have devastating effects on human existence. This is very much like a forced change and seemingly a change that is out of our control.

I'm sure some people would argue that our presence on earth is aiding the rapid climate change that we are seeing. I watched an interesting documentary, *Before the Flood*, featuring Leonardo DiCaprio. One of the interesting statistics shared by one of the scientists was that cows are the biggest contributors to climate change on the planet. It's not via their butts, either; it's through their mouths. They burp an insane amount of times per day. The Environmental Protection Agency estimates that cattle belching and manure management contribute about 28 percent of all anthropogenic methane emissions in the United States, according to Alexander Hristov. As suggested in the film, if people stopped eating beef, climate change would slow down dramatically. Personally, I don't see that happening, as it's a growing billion-dollar industry.

At one point in the documentary, Leo DiCaprio was interviewing the president of Kiribati, Anote Tong, as he was preparing to move his people to an island in Fiji that the country had bought with the intention of relocating everyone. Why, you ask. The sea is consuming the island nation, which is disappearing so fast that the islands may disappear within the next 30 years. That's a massive change to have to deal with, moving an entire nation to another island group. This is a perfect example of a forced change. The people of Kiribati will be forced to raise the islands or move.

4. Forced changes:

In many cases, a lot of changes can seem like forced changes. For example, a woman's boyfriend cheats on her and she leaves the relationship citing that she didn't have a choice. A factory worker hasn't been paid for two weeks and he needs to leave so he can feed his family. A student takes her life as the pressure from her family is too much to handle. The family dog is hit by a car and they have to put the dog down so that it won't suffer. In all of the above examples, you could easily justify your course of action.

And the same could be said for the opposite decision. The woman could give her boyfriend a second chance. The factory worker may well get paid any day from now if he decides to stay. The student could use her situation as a reason to seek counseling. The family could pray and nurse their dog back to health. While we may find ourselves in situations where change seems like the only option, we nearly always have a choice in how we choose to feel about our predicament. If you really think about it that's empowering.

Victor Frankl was an Austrian neurologist and psychiatrist as well as a Holocaust survivor. He is the author of some 20 personal development books. In his book, *Man's Search for Meaning*, he talks about one's ability to change the way one sees and feels about reality even when all liberties have been taken away. It's my understanding that all change can feel forced and it's up to us to choose if that is going to be a tragedy or the best thing that has ever happen to us. We get to choose!

The following quote by Victor Frankl sums up my thoughts on forced changes.

"Everything can be taken from a man but one thing: the last of the human freedoms—to choose one's attitude in any given set of circumstances, to choose one's own way."

5. Intuitive Changes:

Early in this chapter, I shared an example of myself hearing a clear concise voice warning me of an eminent car accident. It's like the feeling of discontent one might have when going through a business transaction. We have these hunches, knowings, gut instincts, and communications with our higher selves, our spirit guides, or even angels. It's within one's ability to be open enough to process and know information that defies logic. Some people call this process following your heart.

When unexpected incidents occur, it really does feel like change just happens to us and we are left to pick up the pieces. You may have found yourself in a similar situation. I would like to share with you a life event that felt like life was happening to me rather than for me.

I was about to move in with my girlfriend of seven months when, on the morning of my birthday, I received a text message from her. She no longer wanted to be with me. I couldn't believe it. By a text message! Who breaks up through a text message? We weren't 16 anymore. Still in disbelief—of all the days it had to be my birthday—I made myself laugh with the thought that she broke up with me on my birthday so she didn't have to buy a gift. She knew I was a speaker. She could have broken up with me through a speech.

I know what you are thinking. John what did you do? Well, we did have a petty argument a few days before. She was at a seminar, and I sent her a message saying I was going to her place to use the internet, which I thought was fine, as there was a blackout in my neighborhood. (This happens in Bali from time to time.) She sent me a message saying that she would be back at 4:30 p.m., but what she meant to say was not to go to her place until she got home.

When she did come home, I was already there on my computer, and she flew off the handle and started yelling, "I told you not to come over to my place until I got home!" And she just went on and on, saying that I don't listen to her. I just couldn't believe what I was hearing. I heard her out and asked her where all of this anger was coming from, and that made her even angrier.

She started bringing up past arguments that I thought we had resolved, and she started calling me stupid. And that was it for me. I calmly told her that obviously something had upset her beyond me going to her place without her permission and that we could talk when she had calmed down. The next day we chatted, and it turned out that she had become jealous when I had spoken with her next-door neighbor. She denied this and kept bringing up things from the past that I thought we had already resolved, and we just kept going around in circles. I explained that it would be best if we didn't move in together just yet, and she agreed. But I guess that upset her more than I thought.

I found myself pointing the finger at her, and I was angry at how could she be so immature. How could she be so childish and hurtful? That had me pondering. When I point one finger at her, there are three fingers pointing back at me. I found myself asking where had I'd been immature, childish, and hurtful. I would never share with her when I was having a difficult day. I rarely spoke from a place of vulnerability and hardly ever shared how I was feeling in any given moment. In hindsight, how could I expect her to open up to me and share from a place of vulnerability?

I realized that she was not the one who had failed the relationship: it was me. This change that I found myself in was my doing, and I had two choices: I could wallow in my sadness or I could help those that were worse off than myself. And, Ding! Like a light bulb, the idea came to me that there are so many orphanages in Bali. There are many children who must feel heartbroken and unloved. I made the decision to visit an orphanage and bring some cheer to children that may feel alone.

When I arrived at Hope Children's Orphanage, I wasn't greeted with doom and gloom at all but with cheer, joy, and happiness. The children started singing "Happy Birthday" to me, and I could feel my heart glowing inside my chest. When you are around children who don't have anything and they live in a humble environment, it's pretty hard to feel miserable, especially when they are singing with such happy, positive spirits.

As I was watching, I noticed out of the corner of my eye a young girl no more four years old sitting on the floor. It felt like she was covered in a blanket of sadness. I walked over while the other children were still singing and picked her up and placed her on top of my shoulders. There was no resistance from her as I began dancing to my tune of the day. Naturally, I moved the little girl's hands to the singing. I could feel her energy begin to shift. The children kept singing more songs, and so I kept dancing with the young child giggling, and some of the other kids were dancing and laughing as well. When I placed her back onto the ground, she was smiling like a well-fed cat grinning from ear to ear.

To think, only a couple of hours earlier I was feeling down in the dumps, and I was amazed at how much my mental state of being had changed after spending time with the children. It shows the power of helping others even when we may not feel like it. You cannot lift another person up emotionally without being affected in a positive way. We can't control how other people respond to us, we can't control others' behavior, but we can control how we respond. This is the same with any situation or change we find ourselves in, we must consider how we respond carefully if we are to navigate changes enamour life successfully.

Chapter 2
Rose-Tinted Specs

By Kay Newton

I am always surprised as I look back on how my life turned out. How did a working-class Yorkshire lass end up living a self-sustained lifestyle in Spain for 30 years, then at the age of 54, move to a small home near a beach in Zanzibar with just 20 kgs of luggage?

I have led a very privileged life, for which I will be eternally grateful. I have been well educated and always had a roof over my head, clothes on my back, love, money, and good health. In fact, I feel a little guilty to have been invited to write a chapter in A Journey of Riches. As a Western boomer child who has everything, what do I have to offer the reader? What gifts can I impart about my discoveries when dealing with changes in my life, and what profound learnings can I share?

I know the riches I have are made of memories, the places I have visited, the people I have met and loved. It may also help that I wear rose-tinted spectacles at all times. You know those specs: the ones that make everything seem better than it actually is and causes you to remember things better than they were. This is my story, my interpretation of the life given to me. So, before I begin, I need you to prepare to journey with me in my shoes and wearing my specs!

Find a comfy place to sit, take a few deep breaths, and imagine placing a pair of the most exotic, expensive, daringly outrageous rose-tinted specs you can imagine on the end of your nose. Now you are ready to read.

My First Pair Of Rose-Tinted Specs: The UK, Innocent Years

My first pair of rose-tinted glasses lasted until my mid-20s. Then the frames became a little too small, very wonky, and of course they were 80s style and, well, not cool anymore!

Born in 1962, I was brought up in a working-class family in the North of England, myself and my younger brother. My father was a factory worker and my mother a school cook. We were a close-knit family. I felt protected and loved. There was always enough, and as a child I was never made aware of the struggles my parents had in providing for us, the extra shifts dad worked or why mum made all our clothes and kept a vegetable garden going all year round. Holidays were spent connected to nature, under canvas, and later sailing in a small boat. We did more than survive; as a unit, we thrived. We all had to work together as a team. Going away each weekend meant we had to be ready at all times. Never was I discouraged from doing anything or from trying out new experiences and learning from them.

I can remember some of those life-changing stages clearly. Call them fate or choices I made. I prefer the word synchronicity.

At the age of nine, I picked up a leaflet just pushed through the letter box and I decided there and then I wanted to do this secretarial typing course for three nights a week at the local village hall. I pestered my parents, who eventually agreed despite the cost and the teacher's reluctance because of my age. For two years, my father helped me carry the heavy portable typewriter to the other side of the village while I dragged a huge cushion to sit on in order to reach the machine. As I did my homework, I learned to type, extended my vocabulary, and widened my general knowledge. Do I remember the bad marks or the tears and pain of the whole experience? Of course not! I was wearing tinted specs! This was the synchronicity which allowed me to not only pass the typing course, but to also pass the 11-plus entrance school exams and to make it through grammar school. Which then led to university, the first in my extended family to do so.

I find that if I listen to my instincts—to that initial gut feeling—things lead to other things. I may not know at the time the reason why I need to say yes or no to something; yet, looking back, I can see the fork in the road where the decision was made.

Another example of intuition and my need to take action was during my 6th Form school year. An opportunity arose to attend a three-week Outward Bound course in the Lake District. No one else seemed interested, and yet the local government was offering to pay. So, I filled in the forms and went. I learned so much about myself, my capabilities within nature, and my love for openness. I still have the written report which sums up my core values, still relevant today: organisation, determination, inspiration, responsibility, conscientiousness, and attentiveness. This has been a true life gift.

Things were not always rosy; no life ever is. We have to take the rough with the smooth in order to learn and grow. Our life is just like a heart monitor with troughs and peaks. When your life is flat it means you're dead!

I was bullied at school. After breaking my ankle in the school gym, I could not attend school for six weeks. When I finally came back, I was ostracised by my classmates and given the name 'Glamour Girl of the Gasworks.' To this day I do not know where the name came from, yet the constant taunting hurt. I spent a few years hiding behind my long hair and seeking friendship at break times with girls from other classes. Despite talking with teachers and my parents, I was left to deal with 'Being sent to Coventry' as best I could, those rose-tinted specs sure came in handy!

That particular pair of specs had to have the tears cleaned off them many a night when my grandmother was dying of breast cancer. Grandma and I had a special bond. I spent many weekends at her house, meeting her friends, attending whist drives, and drinking Horlicks in front of the fire while watching soppy films. Mum brought her into our home. I loved her lots and hated to see her in pain. I felt it was my job to make her laugh and lighten the load. When she died, I put her straight to the back of my mind; yet she resurfaced full throttle many years later during a weekend seminar exercise, and I have rightly put her back where she belongs: in my heart.

University was both fun and hard work at the same time. In those days, the UK government paid the fees. Each term, when my grant cheque arrived, I paid for my studies, accommodations, and books, then divided the remaining amount to cover all other needs. I roughly had enough money to buy a bottle of lager each weekend from the student bar. I left university with no job. Yet I didn't have any debt.

My stubborn character—or was it those rose-tinted specs—refused to take me back home. So, I found a small bedsit and went on the dole while I filled in application forms. I failed to tell my parents about the flatmate below who used to steal my government cheques until the day he committed suicide and was removed in a black body bag. Or about the shared communal toilet nightmare where no one bothered to bring paper with them, preferring to use the walls instead. Or that the only daily meal I ate consisted of scraps donated by the local fishmonger and a cheap bag of rice. This was my life, my choice! My rose-tinted glasses may have been slightly skewed, but I was 21 and wanted to live life on my terms.

I think my parents knew all along. Yet they never interfered or demanded I come home. In the summer of 1983, a chance arose to go cruising along the East Coast of England with a retired couple looking for a yacht crew. Again, without hesitation, I jumped on board, anticipating valuable nautical miles I could add to my yacht master qualifications. We arrived in Whitby in time for the regatta. I had been ashore and stopped opposite the boat mooring to watch a mock Sea-King helicopter rescue, only to find it was, in fact, a real-life tragedy. The diver employed to remove our seaweed issue had not surfaced. It was my first inquest. I didn't wear specs that day.

With heavy hearts, we eventually left port to the Holy Island of Lindisfarne. That evening, as the fast-flowing tides turned, our anchor was tripped by another boat. It took us until dawn to sort it out, and then the owner/skipper collapsed right in front of me from a massive heart attack. I gave him mouth-to-mouth resuscitation for 40 minutes until the helicopter rescue team arrived to take over. He was pronounced dead on arrival at the local hospital. His wife had gone with him and I was left with a boat that needed to be secured and had to find my own way home. With help, practical me did it all, even if I cannot recall how I got home.

I was still in a state of shock when my dad found me curled in a bunk on our small boat at Hull Marina a few days later. He promised me the best thing I could do would be to take the boat out on the next tide to rid me of the memories. What he didn't say was that I would be going alone. With love, he knew this was the best thing I could do; it meant the next stage of my life was secure. Without that experience I would have given up sailing and would not have left for Spain.

But before I can talk about Spain, I have to talk about my three-year career as a baby bouncer! I was eventually offered a job in retail management. I found the work hard and thankless. As a trainee, I often found myself working long hours or taking work home. I was bullied by management, threatened at knifepoint by a customer, and given a commendation by the local police for catching a stalker. Yet my annual reports always said "too nice" to be a manager. They were right: I was not one for bullying others, nor was I one for working inside.

When the sun shone, I used to take my lunch down to the marina and dream. One day my dream came true. A huge boat arrived in Hull going to Mallorca, Spain. Within 24 hours, I had secured a place with the crew, packed in my job, and jumped on board. I never learned to swim back!

My most profound rose-tinted learnings from the UK: There is always enough. Listen to your intuition. Know thyself.

Second Pair Of Specs: Spain, The Ego Years

My new start in Spain, leaving behind my past, yet with my accumulated knowledge and wisdom, allowed me to develop a new state of unconsciousness. I bought a new pair of rose-tinted specs, and it was evident from the beginning that I was going to need them for the next part of my life's journey of riches.

Yet my pair of glasses soon got worn. These were the foggy-lens years when my glasses never seemed to come off, not even for bed. Things happened and the years passed all too quickly: so many stories within a blink of an eye. When I look back, although I have wonderful memories, there was an underlying stress to strive, a need to conform, to fit in, to consume in an accepted Western manner. The years were all about collecting the material things, the trophies, the must-haves. Let me express this clearly. I was in charge of my reality and this is what I wanted to experience; it was my choice.

Here are a few of my stories to share.

Having made the decision to jump on board a 30-meter private motor yacht with three others, men unknown to me, to sail to Mallorca may have seemed naive and reckless at the time. I never would have dreamed of doing so if I had known what was going to happen! Yet taking a risk, opening up to the opportunity, helps us to expand our horizons, knowledge, and character.

My nautical adventure has enough material to deserve its own book. Chapters would include stories about dirty fuel causing the engines to fail in a narrow channel, a lifeboat rescue, bad weather, debris around the propellers, no steering, night fishing boats without lights, drug smuggling, and being stopped by the Spanish Navy. All of these adventures I shared with a retired tanker captain who carried a condom in his top pocket "in case I ever felt the urge," the owner who was addicted to Mateus Rose, and a young pot-smoking friend of the family whose only way back to his parents in Marbella was via the back door.

It took three weeks to travel to the island of Mallorca, weeks in which I grew spectacularly. I found out about the powerful forces of nature, how to trust in others despite their foibles as well as how to trust in a rusty old vessel, how to take control of a life-threating situation (which earned me a commendation from the crew of the Lowestoft lifeboat for remaining calm at all times), and, most importantly, how to call upon my inner strengths and find knowledge I did not know I had in me in order to survive.

My professional life in yachting began in Palma. We moored in the Club de Mar on Friday the 13th, June, 1985, and it was raining heavily. I was truly homesick and wanted to leave. Yet a new phase of the journey had begun, and I now had to learn about becoming a cook and stewardess for the owner's family and wealthy paying chartering guests. All for the princely sum of £50's a week! The experiences, the fun, the laughter, and the memories made up for the shortfall in cash. I can still make an audience laugh as I weave a nautical tale or two into any presentation!

At the end of my first hectic season, having survived long hours hosting, prepping, cooking, cleaning, and sailing, I found myself alone on the boat while the skipper took a holiday in the UK. I will never know what made me jump out of bed in the early hours of the night, but I knew something was wrong. I checked the boat's moorings and found nothing wrong, and so I went to the galley to make tea. By 3 a.m., the winds were gusting 80 miles per hour while green waves and 20-meter boats were coming over the harbour wall as the force of the storm pounded them into the quay. I was in the middle of a hurricane and no one could save me. There was nothing else to do but ride out the storm and trust all would be okay. Bruised and battered the next day, I called the owner, who was extremely angry when I described the damage to his boat. I packed my bags and caught the next flight home. Sometimes you just have to let go of negativity.

Guess what. I got a job back in the UK in retail, playing the old record, the one I hated yet knew all about. Why is it that we love to give ourselves pain until we learn the lesson? Getting a job was easy; letting go for another adventure was a little harder. Yet, I had a plan. Living at my parents' home, I saved as much as I could, and when I reached my target I bought a plane ticket to Hong Kong. A six-week adventure visiting friends, I gained more memories to tell the grandkids.

Back in the UK, I wondered what my life would hold next. It took just 24 hours before synchronicity answered through that mailbox. Would I like to come and work as a cook/stewardess on a boat in Mallorca? This adventure took me to Monaco for the Grand Prix three years in a row, to Corsica, Sardinia, and all around the Balearic Islands. I cooked for self-made millionaires and members of the Spanish royal family. It was hard work, hot 18-hour days and more, but I loved it. Meeting new people, visiting new places, and getting paid in the process—life was good. Yet it wasn't sustainable. My rose-tinted specs were just not working properly. I wanted more: a life partner, a home of my own, kids. And the biological clock had begun to tick in the background.

Synchronicity once again played its hand. It seemed that no sooner had I reached out to the universe and asked for a husband than he was found! The owner of the motorboat I was working on had sold his UK business and bought three flats in a new complex, specially designed second homes for the rich and famous. I moved from the boat and took over running the apartments. My first job was to snag all the faults with the project manager. I met this guy, a project manager, in one of the master bathrooms to discuss the issues which we resolved over dinner, and the man of my dreams was in my life.

As well as beginning a new relationship, I set up a shore-based business and learned a lot about running a company and working for those with a privileged life. Even wealthy people who have it all can be nice, demanding divas, rude, understanding, helpful, nasty, and kind. You name it: they have the traits. Money does not mean that you will have the best relationships or memories. The journey of riches is not one paved with gold bars or dollars. You cannot take any physical things with you when you die.

My fiancé and I planned to elope. We wanted as little fuss about our pending marriage as possible. I did not want to go back to the UK and he did not want to move back to South Africa. Spain became our home. Yet, at that time, neither of us spoke Spanish or wanted the hassle of getting the correct paperwork together for tying the knot in Mallorca. We opted for a registry service in Gibraltar and we told our parents!

So, in my 20s I had partied and worked hard. In my 30s I was running my own business and became pregnant twice. What more could I wish for than to find an old Finca to restore! Our friends thought we were mad. Our first house barbeque was the quickest and quietest ever held. Yet we dedicated the next stage of our life to creating our dream home for our two boys to grow up in. The 11,000 sq m of land with organic veggies, an orange grove, almond trees, chickens, and pets became the centre point of our lives. This was a dream I had always wanted. I worked tirelessly to achieve it and chose this above keeping my guardiannage business going. Our home had a guest house so that grandparents could visit and we could also use it to create an income. I now became a mum, landlady, B&B manager, and organic food grower.

The pace was relentless: constant building, repairing (imagine attempting to breastfeed a new born without a roof on the house and jackhammers in the background), learning about the restraints and rules of living in a new country, learning the language, and finding the fees to pay for private education. Bringing up two boys also had trials, tribulations, rewards, and pride that they brought into our life. The long hours that my husband put in to pay the bills became all too much. Twice he faced depression and almost a complete nervous breakdown, all money related. Yet, he kept on the hamster wheel and I supported his efforts.

We were following our hearts' desires. My most profound lesson through this time was that, whatever reality we create, love can hold it together. These were also times of wonderful love filled with laughter, family, and friends. There is nothing more rewarding than sharing time with your children, and words can never describe the emotions you feel as you watch them grow and thrive. All of their firsts—smiles, walks, days at school, birthdays, special events, sports medals, girlfriends, and memories—I can still see and feel as if it only happened yesterday.

Then one day I wanted more! The house was finished, the boys were growing fast, and I could envision that in the not-too-distant future they would be leaving home. Was this all I wanted to do with my life? Was there not some legacy I needed to fulfill or create before it was too late? I began to train as a personal development coach and created my own brand of Sensibly Selfish coaching for midlife women. I attended expensive life-changing courses, wrote books, learned how to create Wordpress websites, failed as a network marketer and estate agent, and triumphed as European Toastmaster of the year. I seemed to continually strive for the external things in order to understand my purpose in life.

This foggy-spec time continued into my 40s. During this time, as I cared for our family, home, and all of my stuff, I also supported my aging parents. My mother's stroke had left her paralysed, and after she died, my father battled terminal cancer. I spent a lot of time rushing back to emergencies in the UK, leaving my own family to cope as best they could. These were stressful and emotional years, made more pronounced by menopause and the looming empty nest.

I cannot describe the pain I felt having to finally empty the house I had lived in for all my childhood, to remove all of those familiar belongings and re-live the memories while doing so. It was totally draining, the icing on the cake for this stage in my life, and an important lesson for the next, which was just around the corner.

My rose-tinted specs became so scratched and foggy while we were in Spain searching for what; I knew not what. I had become a wife, mother, business person and an orphan. I had lost my children to adulthood and desperately needed to strengthen my relationship with my husband. I no longer wanted the dream lifestyle we had created in Spain, and I wanted to sell the family home so that we did not have to work so hard keeping the ego dream alive and at the same time have my children experience what I had personally just gone through when our time on earth had passed.

My most profound rose-tinted learnings from Spain: Memories are all you have; legacy is what you leave behind. Wealth is LOVE.

New Glasses: Zanzibar, The Wisdom Years and Consciousness

No sooner had we decided to put the house on the market than synchronicity played its next deck of cards. A phone call: would my husband like to be project manager to build a five-star hotel on a pristine beach on the island of Zanzibar? A fitting end to a building career that had begun in Africa. He accepted! I had never heard of Zanzibar before, it was now all about trusting in the process and not worrying about the outcome.

What followed was a hurried period of ditching baggage. This meant letting go of all the things we had accumulated over the past years that no longer served: our home, the physical contents, and any emotional issues. It also meant that other members of the family had to let go, too. One boy was now a chef on a super yacht, following his mum's footsteps, and the other was beginning three years at university studying engineering and alternative energies, following his dad's footsteps. Now they had no home to return to. Home really became "where the heart is."

I also ditched the decision to be a personal development coach. I realised that my clients needed a safe place to vent and let go; yet, at the same time, they needed advice from someone who has accumulated her own t-shirts and ditched her own baggage, something that life coaching does not offer.

With just 20 kgs of luggage, memories, knowledge, and wisdom, it was time to begin a new journey of riches. As they say, the best is yet to come! It was time to get in tune with the next learning curve and focus on exactly how I create my reality.

For me, Africa is so different from my past experiences. It is an assault on all senses. Primal, beautiful, extreme, immediate—these are all words that spring to mind. Stunning sunsets/sunrises over perfect sandy beaches and azure seas, the poverty with grace and happiness, friendliness and the smiles of the local people, overpowering smells, the cacophony of the wildlife, exotic flavours and spices...it is all so breathtaking and emotional.

The excitement of learning a new language, a new culture, eating new foods are all rejuvenating in themselves. It has also created a new set of questions and answers to find. Accepting the way in which the island works, with its traditions and pace of life, is fundamental to fitting in. Yet one thing that stuck out immediately for me was that there is another currency, a culture that surpasses all others, yet something I had carried with me throughout my life without really being aware. No matter where you are in the world, smile! Love rules above all else and we are all made from the same cloth. When you treat people the way in which you wish to be treated, they will reciprocate.

With fewer possessions and a two-room home to live in, I truly learned that less is more. Simple foods will nourish the body, and there is much more time to spend doing the things that I love: beach combing, writing, and spending quality time with my husband.

I had placed rose-tinted glasses permanently upon my eyes and my life has been altered accordingly. I automatically see things in certain ways and fail to see other things. My understanding of my own reality and the way in which I function within it have led me down this path. My life, interactions, and relationships will never be the same because of the choices I made, which at the time were neither good or bad. They were just choices.

The questions that Africa has thrown at me: How can I alter my specs to make sure I get the most out of this third stage in my life? Do I really need rose-tinted glasses now, or is it time to take them off?

I feel this is my greatest challenge yet. I now understand the characteristics and limitations that my sensory apparatus and knowledge have caused me, how my ability to process and interpret their input have compromised my story. Also, how have my cultural expressions from the UK, Spain, and Zanzibar affected the story's outcome? Yet it is no longer about the story.

My journey of riches has now created the next challenge. It is simply not about knowing; it is now time to get in tune with it. Not just to learn to interpret any new data ahead of me from a totally different perspective, but to separate the thing being experienced from the actual experience of it. In essence, it is to work on my consciousness to make it the best I can possibly make it before I leave this world. It is an exciting time, my own Yūgen as it were.

My most profound learnings from Africa: Treat people as you wish to be treated. Less is more. We are all nothing more than consciousness. Just trust in the process.

Your Rose-Tinted Specs

Thank you for reading this far! I hope you have managed to keep your rose-tinted specs on until now. I hope that you have not only enjoyed my story but that it has been inspirational for you as well. At the moment, the world is going through a huge transition from the industrial age into the modern age of technology. This transition has already begun to shrink the world and, at the same time, has made it a turbulent place to live. With uncertainty comes fear; yet deep down we all know that this too shall pass if we just trust in the process. What the world needs right now is more people with rose-tinted specs who can see the good in everything and everyone.

- Are you willing to constantly learn and move comfort zones?
- Can you love and smile more often?
- Do you know yourself and listen to your intuition?
- Are you confident that you will always have enough?
- Have you created wonderful memories that you can cherish, remembering that these are the only things you will take with you?
- What legacy will you leave behind?
- Have you topped up your wealth account with LOVE?

- Do you treat people as you wish to be treated?

- If less is more, what can you let go of right now?

As the world shrinks and cultural blocks break down, we can expect an entirely new set of challenges to appear. The journey of riches lies in not knowing when or how those challenges will be solved, but in just knowing it will be different. So totally different that, as yet, we have no idea what that will be! We may not know in my lifetime, but I do know that my children and my grandchildren will be experiencing the world in a totally different way than I have.

What I do know is that synchronicity will throw something our way and that mankind will have a choice to make. If we are all nothing more than consciousness, trusting in the actual process and not worrying about the outcome is all we can do.

Chapter 3
Tattooed Business Man
By Charlie O'Shea

"You can't connect the dots looking forward; you can only connect them looking backward. So you have to trust that the dots will somehow connect in your future. You have to trust in something—your gut, destiny, life, karma, whatever. This approach has never let me down, and it has made all the difference in my life" ~ Steve Jobs

Please understand I wasn't some super kid that could handle all the troubles in life. I do not want you to believe it was all easy and that all that happened didn't bother me. I just didn't allow all of this to consume me and ruin my life; I became stronger and a better person. My greatest fear for generations to come, with technology moving ahead so quickly and becoming so advanced, is that it will take away children's ability to dream, to visualize, and to imagine.

Back in 2010 when the first iPad was out, Jonathan Nackstrand of the New York Times quoted Steve Jobs speaking about his own children using the iPad: "They haven't used it….We limit how much technology our kids use at home."

Jonathan Nackstrand further quotes;

"Since then I have met a number of technology chief executives and venture capitalists who say similar things; they strictly limit their children's screen time, often banning all gadgets on school nights, and allocating ascetic time limits on weekends."

"Do not allow technology to take away your ability to imagine." ~ Charlie Brown

I remember, when I was a kid, I used to lay in bed and talk to myself for hours, visualizing being rich, having a better life, not being without things, what life was going to be like when I became an adult. Looking back now I realize it was all self-help: spiritually, I was putting my talks out to the universe and the universe was waiting for me to come and collect. Words are a powerful force.

"Do not allow a tragedy or a bad situation in life to define you." - Charlie Brown

At the age of seven I was sexually abused by members of my family, an older cousin, an external family member, and an aunt. Now, I do not in any way want you to think that I encourage or promote this as a business venture, but I want to show you that I did not allow what happened to me to ruin my life. Instead, I turned it to my advantage and created a business! I had the ability to turn an extremely bad situation into a positive, to enable myself to go on with my life and not to be just another statistic of sexual abuse.

My brother, Stephen, was born three months premature. Because of this, he became my father's only child. I was never good for anything. I would get into trouble for things he did, although he knew he shouldn't, but I soldiered on. My father was the only wage earner, and so I had to grow up way beyond my years. There was no time to enjoy childhood. I had to look after both my mom and my brother. My Mother, Christine, was heavily depressed and suicidal. By the time I was 10, she had tried to commit suicide several times. My Father, Carmello (Charlie), found it difficult to look after us and his sick wife, and so we were placed in foster care. I was also placed in various boys' homes. My childhood was spent constantly living way under the poverty line, always renting, moving from house to house, school to school, never settling in one place, never making friends. So, as a child, I had very poor communication skills and was shy towards other children my age.

By the time I was 10, I had decided to run away, and at one time I travelled from Melbourne to Sydney. When I called home for help, my father told me, "You got yourself there; you get yourself back." So, I did. But before I could, I needed money, and that's when I fell into child prostitution, knowing I had something other people wanted.

Because of my home life, even at a young age—around eight years old my business and networking mind began to work. I remember stealing a pass from my school as ID and I took my dad's glass marbles in jars he had been collecting and a book of raffle tickets. So, I set out to make money, and I went door-to-door and sold the tickets. I would say it was for our school raffle. But it didn't stop there. My marketing skills kicked into gear, and I bought more raffle books and took more jars of my dad's marbles. I worked out that if I got four or five friends working for me, and they each sold tickets at 40 cents each, then I could collect 20 cents from every ticket they sold. Then I was making more money.

I remember parents of children that I knew would ask me to steal items for their kids, and they would pay me for doing this. For example, at one time I stole three bikes. I would go into the store and take off all of the labels and tags and ride around the store until security would throw me out with the bike. The even so-called good parents could use me for their benefit. Again, money could be made, and so I did it.

Between the ages of 10 and 16, I spent a lot of my teen years in and out of juvenile detention at either Baltara or Turana. I was living on the streets of Melbourne and Sydney. I started learning to stand up for myself and discovered that by standing over people, using scare tactics and intimidation, I could obtain things I wanted. Now, looking back, I realize that at the time this was the way I felt I needed to be in order to get what I wanted in life. I have since learned to forgive myself, to move on. And I've asked the universe to send love and light to all that I hurt.

In my late teens, I felt that I had to prove something to my father, in a way to win his love, and so I felt that I had to conform to society, marriage, jobs, kids. I met my first wife and got married at the age of 20. Given all of this, nothing much really changed, and I still didn't receive the much sought after acknowledgement I yearned for from my father.

When I was 23 years old, Stephen committed suicide at the age of 21. I felt robbed of life, because I'd had to sacrifice my childhood to help raise him and I'd gotten no acknowledgement from my father. My dad said it should of been me who had died. I felt that everything I had given was all for nothing. At this time, I was in my first marriage and had my daughter Mikayla, who was four months old. Stephen's suicide turned everything back, and nothing was okay.

I worked as a bouncer/security guard and started using drugs. I then realized the money that could be made and which had been made by other drug dealers. So, I quit working the long hours at the nightclub scene on King Street, Melbourne. I enjoyed the work, but I learnt that there was always small-time drug dealers dealing and making five to six times the money I was being paid as a security guard, and I was working 10 to 15 hours per night.

I decided to stop working as a bouncer and take my first step into business. Within a year and a half, I had most of the club scene in Melbourne under my control. Dealers understood that they either worked for me or they weren't allowed to deal at the clubs. I had 30 to 40 dealers working for me.

During this time, my life was consumed by drug dealing and drug using. It wasn't the best business to get into, despite the money I was making. Unfortunately, it's not the best lifestyle, and you cannot switch off just to be a family man. My mum had even become concerned about the sleepless nights. She would tell me to get some sleep, and I would for a couple of hours. Then she would help bag my drugs to distribute. I always found it funny that my mum would break the law so her son wouldn't run himself into the ground. Now, looking back, it was sort of nice to see she cared for me.

My marriage began to fail. I had become self-absorbed and had no regard for being a family man or caring for everyday matters, including appointments or picking up my wife and daughter from places. They would have to find their own way home from appointments and so on. I would miss school plays and family functions. Looking back on that part of my life, I wonder why the hell my wife even stayed with me at all.

At this point in time, I was a heavy drug user. I had started using needles because my nose had collapsed and my doctor said that if I didn't go to needles there was a very good chance I could die at any time with a hemorrhage to the brain. By this stage, there was no way to separate drug dealing, drug using, and being a family man. I ended my marriage, and it had to end on good terms, most importantly, for our daughter's sake. None of this was her fault, and she deserved no further disruption in her life.

Life didn't get any better. I went off the rails in a major way, and my undoing was being arrested and imprisoned for 18 months, with a minimum of 12 months with good behavior. This was my salvation. I got clean and had time to reflect on life and see what I had put my wife, daughter, and mother through. As for my father, at this time in my life I really didn't care about him. One good thing did come out of my going to prison: I have my father's name, and I was on the news and in the paper for the Geelong area where people really didn't know me. Everybody thought that my father had been arrested for drug dealing. I found that to be his karma for all the shit I went through growing up.

I began reading a lot in prison, and this is where I first came across Rich Dad Poor Dad, by Robert Kioysaki, and realized that what my mother used to say was true: if I put five percent of my time into a legitimate business, I would be a success. Once again she was right.

I was released from prison in 2004 and I became aware that I needed to move away from everything I had known in Melbourne. So, I moved to Queensland to regroup and get my life into some sort of order and decide where to from there. In November, 2005, I had to come to Melbourne to visit my daughter and parents. It was at this time that my mother suffered a major heart attack and died at the age of 52.

It's funny how life turns out. All of those years, I had longed for and sought the approval of my father, never receiving it, always being told I wasn't considered a son and that I should have been the one to commit suicide and not Stephen. Only two weeks before she died, I promised my mum that if anything should ever happen to her I would look after my father. So, even though it was a heart attack, I believed she knew something was going to happen to her before Dad, and deep in her heart she knew that I would have just walked away from him, hence the reason she made me promise. So, I moved in with him, and to this day he is still living with me and my new family.

Life stagnated. I found work and just blended into society. I became comfortably numb again. This was what society was about: work, home, then try and save some money for retirement. We are numb flesh, functioning robots, if we just conform to society's beliefs. Looking back, though, I believe universally I needed this time. I then followed the beginning of the technology age and bought my first Mac laptop, and off I went. I ventured into the world of online searching and chat room dating sites. I figured why leave the comfort of my own space.

In hindsight, my mother passing away first was an opportunity for my father and me to rebuild our relationship, not as father and son, but as friends. I am happy to say that we have a relationship today which we never had before. I am glad to say that he is a wonderful grandfather, like the kind of father I wish I'd had as a child.

In 2008, I met Efi and her two beautiful boys: Alexander, 9, and Christian, 6. Soon after, we moved in together and became a family unit with them and my 12-year-old daughter, Mikayla. It was a challenge as far as blended families go, but we did it. There was a reason to create love, unity, and persistence universally in our family home.

I went back and joined the society queue and found a job. I wasn't happy, but given I now had a family, I needed more. It wasn't until I read something my wife wrote in a journal I found—and, no, I didn't know when I opened it that it was an old private journal—and the entry it opened on said, "I don't want to live from pay to pay."

That was the one thing she wanted out of life and from a partner. I guess the universe played its part that particular day and showed me what she put out there, and something had to be done. I never told her that I had read that until two years after we became financially free.

Reading this made me realize that we needed to make more money. My wife encouraged me to find a better job with an employer that wasn't cheating his employees. After a short look, I found a job that paid me more than I had imagined or had ever received legally. My wife noticed that this boosted my self-esteem and she made me ponder that I am worthy of achieving more than I had ever thought I could. Even if I had only chosen to be in a wonderful marriage with great children, I didn't have to settle for average, and my family deserved better than this in life. It was time to kickstart my mind again and create a mindset to reach the next level.

Bali: - thank you for the push.

It wasn't until we took that first family trip to Bali that I was thinking that now I'm 40 years of age and, if we didn't do something about our future, I would soon be 50 and no better off than we were already. I told Efi that I love her and our children so much that it was time to build this empire I had always dreamed of, and that's when my business mind shifted into gear.

I decided that, if I could start a business that would make enough money to pay for our holidays, I'd be happy. Well, I did. It began that way, but it didn't stop there. I told Efi that we were going into business and that we were going to refinance the house. I had 000 ready for the ambulance, as I knew she might have a heart attack (jokingly). After much deliberation and me trying to convince her, our first laundromat was in planning mode, and so I started reading books on how to borrow money for financing, how to set up, and so on and so on. During all of the planning and negotiations, going back to the family unity and the universe, the beginning of our family business name was conceived:

ACCME

Efi told me we should call it ACCME being the acronym for Alex, Charlie, Christian, Mikayla, Efi.

Believe in the universe; it has its reasons.

I plucked up enough courage and told Efi that I was going to ask her father for a small loan to cover the amount we were short. A heartache did follow, as she didn't want to borrow from her mother and father. She made me promise that I wouldn't ask them. I kept my promise, or rather part of it. I just altered it and didn't ask them together. I only asked her father.

Once again, we did it. The business was up and running, and in under a year I again had 000 ready on the line. With our AUS emergency services on standby, I announced to Efi a second shop and even more debt this time. I am happy to say that both businesses are thriving now. We knew it was about giving people what they wanted and to be able to enjoy the experience. We both come from customer service backgrounds, and so we knew what we had to give to our customers. The biggest mistake most business owners make is that they build a business and expect it to run on its own. You need to dedicate 200% and get to know your customers and their needs. You will need to do this especially in the first five years. I will not lie: there are hard times in those first five years, but with solidarity and commitment you do get through them. You need to persevere in order to be successful.

Back to Bali: our second trip. Again, thank you, Universe, as on our first trip we were sent the most beautiful soul on earth, Ketut Eliex. Ketut was not the original driver we had booked the day we met him. Instead, he was asked to help his employer, who had been double booked. We hit it off like it was meant to be. Ketut became our family, along with his extended beautiful family, whom we have chosen to help out financially. His father was saving for a new boat, as this is part of their livelihood. Bali doesn't have any assistance for the elderly and the retired. If you don't work, you don't eat. It's that simple! We decided that we would help with purchasing the boat; we could speed the savings along. Not long after we hot back from Bali, the new boat was bought, it was named *Charlie Brown & Shanti. (Shanti,* means "peace" - Peace in body, speech and mind.) in Sanskrit.

Another business idea began to formulate, mainly for two reasons. First, our second trip, which happened to be in January, a season of extremely high humidity, our clothes took almost one and a half weeks to dry. Second, we had an opportunity to also have Ketut to build a business with us through partnership, in order to provide for his family and not have them to worry for the rest of their lives.

It's funny how the universe opens the doors in life. Before this point, we wouldn't have been able to open a business internationally. Also, who could you trust to run and maintain that business? Because of Indonesian laws, in order to have a business in Bali, we would need a partner that was Indonesian born. Ketut said he would love to work for us, but when we told him this news, he was sad, because he knew he would not be able to afford to buy into the business. I explained to him that we had already thought of that and not to worry—we would put up the money for the business and he would run and maintain it. We knew that with the money he would be making not only would he look after his family but his whole village. Money isn't evil. It only amplifies the person you already are.

Do not let what's inside you waste away. Do not allow others to tell you that you cannot do something.

I knew from my school days that I had ideas and that I was smart and had business skills. I could do many things and succeed, but I allowed society to bring me down throughout my early life, without the support and encouragement from my parents to help me strive at something. I remember in grade five my teacher made me stand in class while she proceeded to say that in her 30 years of teaching she had never had a child as slow as me. She didn't understand why I tossed the desk at her after that comment.

Analyzing my school years, I now know I was dyslexic! You have to understand that back in the 80s, and even the 90s, dyslexia was not openly recognized. Nowadays it may appear as though we have caught up with the times. It's not perfect, but it's not as bad as it was back than. I do not allow this hurdle to stop me from reading and educating myself in my own way. So, again, this is not a hindrance. You can embrace this and learn to overcome it, too.

Our youngest son, Christian, has Asperger's. However, we did not allow him to believe that this would in any way stop him from being the best he can be in life. We encouraged him to believe in what he wants and to read books. He has been reading financial books since he was 12. He's 15 now. Because he is a reader, his many difficult school years (thanks to our never changing school system) have not kept him from believing that he can achieve what he wants in life. He now wants to go to business school and eventually to take over and run the family empire. So, again, here is another example of not allowing society to dictate to you what you should be in life.

However big or small your dream, like *NIKE* says, "Just do it." Do not allow any tragedy in your life to consume you and waste your life away. Control the events in your life; use them to your advantage and gain power from them. Many people get to live to a ripe old age but spiritually die in their 20s. There are so many dreams and hopes that lie in the graveyards. We are a product of our own making.

The rules of the game:

I believe that the universe, gods, or even Mother Earth—whichever is your preference—did not intend for us to suffer and live in constant anxiety and fear of the future. I believe that life is a game and, once you open your mind to see the bigger picture, you will understand that it's only a game. After we understand this, life becomes so enjoyable. One must first learn that, without understanding this basic principal, moving forward is not possible.

Learning to forgive yourself is one of the first things you must do. How can you ever forgive others if you can't forgive yourself? Then, learning to love yourself is one of the hardest but necessary things a person can learn to do. Growing up in this world of false hopes we learn from magazines, television, and other media sources. We are given the perception that what is printed or shown is how we should all strive to be. This falseness poisons the mind and the spirit. Life is a game. If we play the game and learn the rules, it should all fall into place. I also believe that, because our parents were educated through the industrial age, they had no understanding of how to move away from society's beliefs and programming. They followed what their parents taught them and so on, being no better off than what their parents were.

In life, magic happens when we allow things fall into place. Once you start to let go of the wheel that you have been trying to control all your life and trust that things happen for a reason, don't be afraid to fail, for that is a learning process. You can than learn the lesson and grow.

Here is an example of how the universe works when you voice your desires. Back in 2013, I announced to the universe that I would someday like to write a book. The timing happened to be right as we neared the end of 2016. This was when I met John Spender, who happened to get in touch with me. We did not know each other before this and were from two different places in the world. John is the author of *A Journey of Riches* and allows co-authors to share their stories. So, here I am with this blessing that the universe has offered. I grasped the opportunity with open gratitude and thankfulness. My dyslexia cannot stop me from accepting this very special opportunity. So, with the help of my beautiful wife, who is also my best friend, we got to work.

What I am sharing with you is not to impress you. It's to have a favorable effect on you. Through my family's journey with me in the past three years, we have started two successful businesses and have more plans for 2017. We are in the process of building our first partnership in Melbourne with good and like-minded friends, completing our fourth independent business in Melbourne. And we are also venturing forth internationally with our first business in Bali, with many more to come over there. We have also started on the path of building a network marketing business, which has taken off nicely. We believe it will become another passive income stream.

I'll say a little about network marketing. You need to be open-minded with regards to this. Pre-judging a book by its cover is basically giving up, not being open to possibilities that have been proven to work. People are scared of a commitment that can work based on what their friends or family think. "It's a scam," "these things only make the person on the top wealthy," etc. NO. Open your mind to learning about this. Then, and only then, when you have all the facts you should make your OWN judgement.

Let me put this another way. You willingly give your internet or phone provider a monthly fee to access the world, Yes? Well, apart from keeping up to date with the Kardashians, what other benefit do you personally get from this? Nothing. You are making CEOs and shareholders richer than ever before. So, be open to something that may make you passive income, and in the worst case, you have fun.

Great things lie ahead for all who believe.

I hope that my story may have impacted and inspired you toward a change in thinking about life's opportunities, or that it has at least sown a seed to ripen when your time is right. The universe is made up of vibrations. Start sending out the right vibrations so that you can start receiving what you and your family truly deserve. Start improving your mindset with reading, videos, podcasts, and so on. Start feeding your mind and watch it grow, but never forget that knowledge without action is only knowledge. You must take that leap of faith to turn it into action.

A dream will always remain a dream until you turn that dream into a goal and then start working towards that goal until it comes to pass. Then that goal becomes your reality.

Chapter 4
Lost And Found

By Chris Drabenstott

"I once was lost, but now I'm found; I was blind but now I see."

Now, THAT'S some Amazing Grace.

Nothing like being overweight, jobless, depressed, alcoholic, always seeking a man's approval, and feeling separated from God to learn how it feels to be lost. Lost is where I found myself at a dark and lonely place called rock bottom a little over a year ago. My losses were what took me there, and Grace is what brought me out.

Grace…what an amazing and beautiful gift.

I learned some things during that visit to rock bottom. I learned that losing things isn't all bad. It's just a natural part of the most constant thing that exists in life: CHANGE! I learned that sometimes you have to lose some things in order to find something better. That's what I call a lose/win situation. And, as I reflect back over the past year of my life, I've had some pretty significant losses that have led to some even greater wins. I also learned that, if we never get lost, we can never know the feeling of peace and purpose that settles into our souls during the process of finding our way back to our Divinely-inspired path.

If you're reading these words, you've likely experienced some of those lose/win situations yourself, and that's simply because you are human. We all experience them. I'm not just talking about physical losses or things you can touch. In fact, often the most powerful losses are of the emotional and spiritual kind that are the catalysts for the greatest changes that lead us right back to Grace, which is the ultimate win in life.

It was only a few days before the ringing in of a new year, and as I passed through the meditation room in my house, I paused in front of my vision boards to do a quick assessment of the things that needed to be taken down and replaced with new dreams and fresh visions. I noticed on one of my boards a photo that I had cut out of a *Travel & Leisure* magazine depicting a peaceful aquamarine infinity pool surrounded by palm trees, with a caption that read, "Where Will You Go This Year?" I smirked a little, feeling a bit prideful as I thought about the massive year of change that was almost behind me, which included journeys to some pretty awesome destinations.

I panned upward and noticed another magazine cut-out picturing a man hang gliding across a wide open blue sky in the middle of a vast desert with a smooth blanket of caramel-toned sand and "Free Your Soul" boldly captioned across the bottom. The man in the photo appears to be on the verge of landing at any moment. As I studied the ad, I found myself trying to imagine the thoughts that might be bouncing around in his head as he glided through the warm desert air and drifted effortlessly in the dead silence. I pondered, "What in the world is he going to do when he eventually touches down in the middle of that scorching hot empty desert, able to see only sand and sky as far as his eyes can see? How will he feel as he looks into the distance in every direction and realizes that he has nowhere to go and no one to help him find his way?" The truth was, I knew exactly how he'd feel: lost.

Being lost and feeling alone have become concepts that are more than familiar to me. In fact, over the course of my life I've come to know them quite intimately. When we're physically lost, we're unable to see the correct or acceptable course. We lack direction. We can't seem to find our way. When feeling emotionally lost, we struggle to see the right decisions to make. And when something that belongs to us is lost, we either lose it forever, or, at some point, we end up going back to find it again.

In my elementary school, there used to sit a tattered cardboard box with a piece of paper taped to it with the words **Lost and Found** written in thick black marker. In this box were all of the hats, gloves, scarves, and belongings that were at some point left behind and forgotten. Day after day, these items became part of a bigger and bigger junk dump, awaiting their owners to come back and reclaim them. As I was staring at the hang-gliding man on my vision board, I began to think about my own personal junk dump and started pinpointing a multitude of things that I had lost over the course of my life thus far, some of which I went back to reclaim and others that were clearly better left behind.

I Lost My Job and Found My Purpose

An interesting but not so uncommon thing happened to me at age 45. I lost my job. I found myself in the middle of a life crisis that leaves many in a state of utter panic. I had been in management with this company for almost a decade, and so I had participated in the unfortunate conversations that precede the proverbial pink slip. But I had always been the one delivering the bad news, not the one receiving it. When it was my turn to be let go, I remember hanging up the phone in a state of disbelief. How could this be happening to me? Almost immediately I called my closest confidant to share what I then believed to be my terrible misfortune. The call went something like this:

"Hey…um…(awkwardly long pause)…I just lost my job."

"Are you serious? Are you okay?"

"Um…I dunno. I think so. Maybe I'm still in shock, but strangely…I feel fine right now. I was preparing for a good, long cry but nothing came out. It probably just hasn't hit me yet."

In hindsight, I know why I handled the situation so gracefully. Although I had no idea at the time, I was entering the very beginning of what the great Dr. Wayne W. Dyer refers to as my "afternoon," otherwise known as that terrifying, yet beautiful and defining phenomenon that typically happens a little later in one's lifetime when the sun begins to set, the world gradually quiets, and we're overtaken by a dusk of contemplation about our true purpose in life. Who am I? Why am I here? What am I supposed to be doing with my life?

The door to my 20-year career in corporate technology had just been slammed in my face, and rather than being overtaken by panic and worry, I felt only a strange sense of peaceful relief. Fortunately, a decent severance package afforded me the luxury to do something that I had never previously done in my life: think about what it was that God has put me on this earth to do.

In high school, we're prepared (I use that term loosely) for college by taking placement exams and meeting with someone anointed with the title of Guidance Counselor, whose "guidance" generally consists of reviewing the test scores and asking a few simple questions about what type of career we think we'd like to pursue. The truth is, after we've flung our graduation caps high into the air, eager to make our marks and conquer the big bad world out there, we really have no doggone clue as to where the overly anticipated path of adulthood will lead us. Take my path, for instance. I graduated from college with a B.S. in Psychology and had planned to open my own clinical practice of Christian counseling to help other people with their problems. I spent my first several post-grad years in social work, experiencing the dismal burnout rate, lack of income potential, and the realization that I had a tough enough time dealing with my own problems, let alone those of others. So, I decided to pack up my life and move to the bright lights and big city of Chicago, where I took a job selling scissors, which then led to a sales job in technology, which is the career that shaped the past twenty years of my professional life that had now come to a screeching halt.

Enter my "afternoon." And probably the biggest aha moment of my life. During this time, I realized that virtually my entire career in technology was never really my idea! Day after day, as I took another bite out of my severance money, I was mulling over the big life questions. How could I have wandered off my path into a profession that I didn't even choose? How could I have fallen into the trap of helping someone else live out their dreams instead of pursuing my own? How did I not know better? How could I have been lost for twenty years?

We're all born with a spirit that acts as an inner compass, that, when properly connected, provides us with spot-on directions to wherever we're trying to go. I discovered that, although not lost forever, somewhere along the way my inner compass had been misplaced, and the time had finally come for me to go back to that cardboard lost and found box to reclaim it. For so many years, I had relied upon everyone else for directions instead of finding my own way. Driving down the road of life, I took this turn and then that turn, following directions that told me: go straight for five years, then get off at the exit marked *Someone Else's Dream,* and continue down that road until you see a big sign that says *Dead End.* Then, once you realize that you're good and lost, make a U-turn and go back to where you came from.

I had blindly followed everyone's directions but my own, although there lived an intuitive GPS inside of me all along. I like to call that device my SPS (Spiritual Positioning System). We all know that subtle feeling that arises from deep down in our gut that tries to sound the alarm when we're veering too far off course. The problem comes about when we've never been taught how to recognize this intuitive part of our spirit, and, moreover, how to build the confidence to actually listen to it and muster the courage to follow it. Recognizing it, listening to it, and following it are the steps to learning how to jump.

There's a video circulating on social media of a short talk by Steve Harvey that mentions this very concept. He paints the picture of jumping off a cliff when faced with those moments that happen during your "afternoon" and trusting that, even though we might experience some serious scrapes, bumps, and bruises on the way down, God has given us a divine promise that our parachute is guaranteed to open and safely support and guide us as we fall. But if we never find the initial courage to jump, we'll never know the incredible blessings of the Great Mystery that await us, both in the midst of our fall and ultimately when our feet touch the ground.

As a young woman, I was never taught how to feel the familiarity of my God-given gifts and talents. I missed the memo on how to connect with them in my spirit and how to feel gratitude for them. I know now that our gifts aren't randomly distributed; they are specific and unique to each and every one of us. And, when followed, they will lead us right into a life filled with passion, purpose, and connection to our Divine Source. What we may consider to be the most trivial of gifts may very well be the solid clues we're searching for that will connect us with our true reason for being on this earth. But, as the saying goes, you just don't know what you don't know.

Professionally, instead of directing my attention inward toward my gifts, I looked at the things that were found on the surface. Money. Promotion. Status. Title. I allowed those things to define who I was, and, as a result, I ended up lost, following the directions of others instead of my own SPS. I spent two decades drifting from job to job in whatever direction the wind was blowing. Bishop T.D. Jakes has been quoted as saying, "If you can't figure out your purpose, figure out your passion, for your passion will lead you right into your purpose." And the way to finding your purpose is to recognize, listen, follow, then JUMP!

With a resume full of experience in technology and a quickly dwindling severance package, rather than backing away from the ledge, I made the courageous decision to leap right into my afternoon by leaving the corporate world behind and discovering a whole new world of Network Marketing. It was as if a switch was suddenly flipped and I was ready for adventure! Ready to take risks! Ready to live life on the edge! Ready to feel anything but safe. Ready to discover the real me and my unique spiritual gifts. I had reclaimed my inner SPS and I knew that my life was about to get redirected in a major way.

I Lost My Ego & Found My Identity

For as long as I can remember, I've had an identity that included being overweight. I was also smart, funny, personable, athletic. And just chubby enough on the outside to feel fat and unworthy on the inside. It seems that every time I'd lose some weight, it was inevitable that I'd end up finding it again. When I was young, I did what most girls did: I compared myself to every other girl. The voice inside my head was hard at work. "Her thighs are so long and skinny." "Her stomach is so flat." "She must be a size zero." "I could never fit into those jeans." Thus, my shallow ego was being strengthened, tricking me into the idea that worthiness and acceptance depends primarily on the values of society and the naked eye, physical appearance, and outer beauty.

I mean—let's be honest here—perfect-looking people are plastered all over every movie screen, magazine cover, and commercial, taunting us to criticize and over-examine every ounce of our being. If no one is there to teach us about self-love and the true identity of the spirit inside of us, what else is there to believe in? Scrutinizing my body became a daily event that set the stage for years of self-esteem hurdles that had me running into relationships that had no hope of surviving. I have spent a lifetime of building a belief that I was never enough. I consider myself a victim of identity theft, stolen by a criminal who goes by the name of Ego.

Rewinding back to that high school cap and gown era, I was an elite athlete with a promising college volleyball career ahead of me. At five foot, four inches, 145 pounds, I should've been happy with my strong, healthy body; yet, all of my friends seemed so much skinnier than me. I used sarcastic humor and my ability to read people's personalities to gain acceptance. My savvy knack for tapping into others' psyches and adapting my own behavior according to what made them feel comfortable was a gift that won me the popularity I was yearning for. But it was the way that I allowed Ego to cultivate a garden of shame and self-doubt that set the stage for my future.

In my freshman year of college, each volleyball teammate was required to weigh in and have her body fat percentage measured on a regular basis. Trying to fend off the "freshman fifteen" to maintain an acceptable playing weight became what felt like a life or death mission. If you're too fat, you could lose your starting position, and potentially even your scholarship. At least those were the threats at the time. What started earlier in life as a means of subconscious comparisons and mind chatter had now risen to a whole new level of scrutiny.

Approaching my sophomore year of college, I decided to transfer to a different university and was invited by the coach to visit the new campus on a weekend that the team was hosting a tournament. At the pinnacle of my visit, I can still vividly remember sitting in his office, my mom in the chair beside me, full of hope that he wanted me on his team. He did. And he had a full athletic scholarship to offer me to boot! Beaming with pride, I absorbed my new coach's welcoming, kind words, and we sealed the deal with a firm handshake and a smile. He slid the contract across the desk and I signed on the dotted line, and he said, "Now, when you come back in the fall, I want you to show up at 150 pounds." This meant I'd need to lose 12 over the course of that summer.

AGAIN with the weight? At age 20, it was still haunting me, this never-good-enough-never-skinny-enough devil on my shoulder, which remained with me throughout the rest of my college years and well beyond. As a matter of fact, within a year after I had graduated from college, I had tipped the scale at 202 pounds. From then on, my entire adult life has been cursed with the weight loss yo-yo: gaining some, losing some, gaining more, losing less. By age 40, I was a hopeless, self-loathing 100 pounds overweight and made the desperate decision to have gastric bypass surgery. In less than a year's time, I had shrunk to a proud, petite 138 pounds, adorning a size 4 jeans, a size I hadn't seen in 30 years!

What I failed to consider was that Ego wasn't about to shrink the way I had. In fact, it was stronger than ever. Despite looking and feeling amazing, my mind was still judging, disapproving, and holding my true identity in handcuffs. "Who am I now?" I wondered. For all practical purposes, my identity as I knew it had been hijacked since elementary school; I never really knew who I was. Now, I had lost the weight, but I had done nothing to find my soul. The emptiness that I had always tried to fill with comfort food could no longer be filled the same way, as my post-surgery stomach was about the size of a golf ball. My love affair with food ended like an abrupt break-up that you never see coming. Poof! One day you're blissfully in love, and the next you're sleeping next to the dog.

Still uncomfortable with my emptiness, I began to fill my soul-void with alcohol. Wine, to be specific. It was the perfect rebound. My stomach stayed full, my emotional pain was numbed, and I looked like a million bucks! As the next several years passed, I found myself filling up with about three bottles of wine a day, seven days a week. And then the unimaginable happened: the weight started creeping back on. I justified the climb by thinking that a five-pound gain could be chalked up to water retention. A 10-pound gain was considered to be predictable, normal, and even acceptable for gastric bypass patients. But within three years of my 100-pound weight loss, I had gone back to that elementary school cardboard box to reclaim almost half of the weight that I had lost, and what I found as an added bonus was the inability to stop drinking. Yep, I was now the proud owner of the label "alcoholic."

I was sinking fast. And just when I thought things couldn't get much worse, I received that pink slip call from Human Resources telling me that my services would no longer be needed. I was forced into my afternoon. I use the word "forced" because it's the only word that can describe what it feels like to be pushed toward the edge of the cliff, bringing you face-to-face with one of those life-changing leaps that can either make or break your destiny. I had a challenging choice to make. I could throw up the white flag of surrender or I could have "the angry talk" with myself; you know, the kind of talk that a trainer has with his boxer when he's getting pummeled by the other guy in the ring. The bell dings at the end of the round and the boxer stumbles back to his stool, bloodied, leaning back against the ropes with arms stretched out wide, gasping for air, unsure which decision is the lesser of the two evils: finishing the fight or throwing in the towel. I like to refer to those kinds of talks as a small doses of encouragement, followed by a stiff jab-cross-uppercut combination, where the only thing left to do is put the mouthpiece back in and reach deep down inside to find your spiritual gangster.

Growing up, whenever I wasn't pushing to reach my potential, my parents used to say to me, "you better shape up or ship out!" So that's exactly what I did: I shaped up. After seeing a weight loss transformation photo of a friend on Facebook, I called her up and asked her to share with me how she did it. Her one-word answer sent me into the most impactful change of my life thus far: Isagenix.

Overweight, alcoholic, jobless, depressed, and lost, I knew that the time had come for me to jump; but what I didn't know was how that jump would forever change the course of my life. I pulled together the money to start consuming these nutritional products and lost 40 pounds in four short months. In return, I found a culture of uplifting people who inspired me to get back into the fight for my life. With products that had me feeling and looking amazing again, I found my footwork to get back into that ring.

My next opponent: the bottle. In the course of joining Alcoholics Anonymous, I lost my dependency on wine to fill my soul, and, as a result, I found my second wind. In the course of walking away from the land of corporate America and faithfully pursuing the network marketing opportunity that was placed so timely right in front of me, I lost the feeling of unfulfillment, and in return I found a way to start living my dreams. Before I knew it, I was dancing around the ring, and I had Ego dangling helplessly on the ropes. THIS is who God meant for me to be— a fighter forced into her afternoon, ready and willing to take the biggest jump of her life because her faith was bigger than her fears. Anais Nin claims that "life shrinks or expands in proportion to one's courage." Because of what was to come next, my life was getting ready to expand beyond what I could've ever imagined.

I Lost My Religion & Found My Relationship

My search to find the right religion has been ongoing since childhood, and it has now come full circle. Like many kids, I grew up in a church-going family, participating in vacation Bible school and Christian youth camps because that was just what people did. By the time I had reached college age, I had stopped going to church altogether until a few years after I had graduated, when I began my search for God again. I felt like somewhere along the way, I had lost him. My life was moving along with no complaints, but there still grew inside me a subtle knowing that something important was missing.

I began searching for a sense of deep fulfillment and purpose for my life and was certain that, if I could just find a church that was the right fit for me, it would help me to locate the answer to that big question of "Why am I here?" Quite methodically, I set out to visit a new church every week until I found the one that suited me best.

Conveniently, my first visit was to an Episcopalian church that was walking distance from my downtown Chicago brownstone apartment. The service was full of liturgy and doctrine that resembled some of the Catholic services that I had been to before, but it wasn't for me. It was too rehearsed, too stiff, too prim and proper. After that came visits to Lutheran, Non-denominational, and eventually a Baptist church that surprisingly became my church home. I remember driving past the massive, white stone church with my roommate at the time and blurting out, "Hey, is that a Catholic church?" She replied, "Naw. I think it's Baptist." I followed up by asking her if she knew anything about the Baptist denomination, and she chuckled, "Yeah, just a little bit. My dad's a Baptist minister!" Because of the multicultural nature of the area that we were living in, I had made the assumption that the congregation would be fairly diverse. Wrong! I'll never forget that Sunday morning when I walked through the tall arched doors and found not another white person in sight. Not that it bothered me in any way.

As I approached the wide staircase leading up to the sanctuary that was covered in garnet red carpet, the massive, thunderous sound of the historic Kimball pipe organ vibrated deep into my soul. Up the staircase I went, curiously peering into the sanctuary when I reached the top, which was a giant, two-story horseshoe, shaped like a big hug that wrapped around its congregants. Having always been involved in singing growing up, I instantly connected with the spirited harmony of the gospel choir that had the entire congregation on its feet, clapping in unison and joyfully singing along. No one seemed to be concerned about what the person next to them was doing, or how they were worshiping, or following any unwritten rules. Everyone was free to express themselves to God in their own unique way, which is something I had never seen in church before.

Then came time for the sermon. The pastor stepped up to the lectern, and he reminded me of King David in the story of David and Goliath: small in stature, but mighty in character. He was a Biblical scholar and theologian who devoted his life to learning and teaching the Word of God, but most of all, he was a passionate, respected leader who led with his heart. He taught me that Christianity should be thought of as a relationship, not a religion. He taught me that sometimes the mysteries of the Bible will challenge you to "chew the meat and spit out the bones" in order to recognize what rings true in your heart. What I found in this church was, the more I studied, the hungrier I was to learn more. Sunday morning service soon led to Wednesday night Bible study class, and not long after, I found myself visiting local seminaries and enrolling in a graduate program to study Divinity.

As the word got out, I was often asked excitedly, "Are you going to be a preacher?" And without hesitation I'd reply, "Oh, no, no...I just want to learn more about the Bible." In my mind, I was really just after more knowledge and believed that I should follow the Bible's instruction to "study to show thyself approved." The truth is, the girl who was never enough was petrified by the possibility that preaching God's Word might actually be part of her purpose.

Despite working a full-time job, I discovered that sitting in seminary class as an eager-to-learn student lit a fire deep inside of me, a fire for words, stories, truth, meaning, and the self-discovery that I was finding inside of the endless puzzle of Biblical scripture. In my third year of seminary, the time had come to take some preaching classes as part of the curriculum. The inevitable became a reality. I preached several times at my own church and was asked to be a guest preacher at other churches. I actually believed myself to be quite good at bringing Biblical stories to life.

But something in my spirit was still off. I couldn't understand it. I was doing all the right things: studying, praying, serving in the community, and building my personal relationship with God. So why did I still feel so lost? I've heard it said that when you go to seminary, you better be careful not to lose your faith. I suppose this is because the knowledge that's accumulated opens the door for you to really think for yourself and to fully examine, and consequently to often doubt and/or refute, what was previously accepted as Truth according to our spiritual teachers.

The deeper I dug into knowledge, the more I found myself chewing on that meat that my pastor talked about, conflicted with trying to reconcile Biblical truth with the truth that was growing inside of my own heart. As I began to spit out more and more of those bones of false truths, I discovered that the flame that had once burned so strongly inside of me began to dissipate until I was no longer preaching or even stepping foot inside the church. I had convinced myself that I would find God in my own unique and individual way that felt comfortable and genuine. Instead, several years passed in the blink of an eye, and other than the occasional church program on television, I wasn't seeking out spiritual development much at all. My life became more about getting ahead in my professional career than finding a deeper purpose in life. I had lost my faith.

Here's where everything comes full circle. When I leaped into my new career of network marketing, I experienced one of those lose/win situations. With Isagenix, I was able to lose the weight that I had found after my gastric bypass surgery, and, in the process, I became a part of a tribe of like-minded business builders who were not only involved in the business of sharing the best health products on the planet, but were also immersed in the business of self-discovery. I had found my new congregation: a fellowship of spirited, soul-seeking, success-driven entrepreneurs who shared the vision of changing the world on a massive scale. And just like that, my SPS had course-corrected and I was right back on track.

If it hadn't been for all of my losses, I wouldn't be finding myself where I am right now. If it weren't for my weight loss, I wouldn't have found my health with the products of Isagenix. If I hadn't lost my job, I wouldn't have found a most rewarding career in network marketing, which not only pays my bills but--more importantly--feeds my ministry.

I don't regret my losses; I am grateful for them. Being led back to my relationship with God and discovering my true identity has been an immeasurable gift. I no longer seek approval by trying to be enough, neither through relationships nor through the eyes of anyone but myself. I've learned that filling that empty space inside can only come from nourishment of the soul.

When I made the decision to take the jump into network marketing, I chose the same strategy that had helped me to achieve success in corporate America: finding a mentor! Getting into a position to build solid work relationships and learning from the best was a skill that I had been honing for many years, and my strategy for network marketing was no different. Although at the time I thought that I was seeking out a mentor for my new business, what I found blew that expectation out of the water. Her name is Casey. And she was my parachute.

Casey did fulfill my initial expectations; she mentored me from a business standpoint and shared everything she knew about how to become a millionaire and live the life you've always dreamed of. What I wasn't prepared to find was an angel on earth, who, through close personal and spiritual development mentoring, would direct me back to my inner SPS, which had been turned off for most of my life, and ultimately put me en route to my destination of my true higher Self. It's been just over a year since I jumped into my afternoon, and with every new day the fall from that jump is filled with experiences that lead me to become more awakened, more purposeful, more blissful, and more enlightened.

I've found a network marketing company worth aligning with, whose slogan is "Solutions that Transform Lives." And transforming lives is precisely what I'm now mentoring others to do through my own global health and wealth business. As a team leader of the YACHT Club, I am able to live out the "YACHT" acronym every day as I preach the vision of "You Are Called to His Team."

I've lost the blinders of my Ego so that I can see the light-beaming truth of my spiritual identity. I've learned that our bodies do not define who we are, and the only way that we can transform unhealthy bodies into healthy ones is to master the love of self. If we don't fully love and accept who we are as a divine spirit, we will surely go back to the lost and found junk dump to reclaim what we've lost, and continue the dreaded weight yo-yo. I've started a Facebook support group called LiveFULLy, which provides hope, encouragement, and optimal nutrition for those who share in my struggle with severe obesity and compulsive overeating. We have incredible online support and education, and everyone is welcome. It is my sincere belief that owning my FULL story is necessary in order to have the capacity to lead others on their journeys to discovering their true identities.

Finally, I've lost the boundaries that I used to keep my religion confined to, and in return I'm sailing through that wide-open sky like the hang glider on my vision board, with eyes wide open to the expanded possibilities that encompass all people and all things as inherently One. This new perspective has led me to fulfill a long-time dream of writing a book with a premise that is centered around the internal power of the SPS that we all possess to heal ourselves and one another. By exploring the chakra system and how it can be better understood in conjunction with various healing modalities, I am working on a manual to help identify and release acquired soul ties that hold us back from living out our fullest, most enlightened spiritual lives.

Enough about me, let's talk about you! Are you in a dead-end job, searching for a career that will allow you to live a purposeful life on your own terms? Have you already programmed your inner SPS, or do you still find yourself allowing others to control your destination? Do you struggle in differentiating your true self from the person that your Ego has tricked you into believing you are? I know that if this book has found you, You Are Called to His Team, and all things are possible for you, just as I am now seeing my heart's desires being manifested in my reality.

A dear friend and Reiki master once offered me an affirmation to recite aloud when I would find myself feeling lost. It states, "I find and know my true self. I allow joy and happiness to be a daily event." I've come to the conclusion that sometimes you have to lose your way in order to find yourself. Be grateful for the losses in your life that are allowing you to find the amazing grace that's available if you'd only find the courage to jump. We can all be parachutes for one another during the fall, helping each other to find the inner light that will lead us out of the darkness and into the *journey of riches* that awaits!

Chapter 5
'Change'

By Theera Phetmalaigul

It was a cool morning in December of 2016 in Bangkok, Thailand, the country where I was born and raised. This particular morning, I had time to ponder back over the past few years of my life. It had been an amazing four years since I'd left my full-time job as regional manager of the biggest oil companies in the world. I had been working with ExxonMobil since 1993, right after I graduated as a young mechanical engineer, and I had worked my way up the corporate ladder. With discipline and hard work, after a good 19 years with this company, I had become Regional Manager in the Finance/Controller Division. Being the first Thai national to achieve this high position made me and my family very proud.

I was born in a small province called Phetchaburi, about two hours south of Bangkok. As a countryside boy raised in a Thai/Chinese family, I was taught to study hard, to find a good secure job, and to just stay on until retirement. I think this is a common goal for Asian parents who went through economic recession. My Dad actually was a great entrepreneur and my role model. I remember that he had a mega real estate project that could have made us very rich if it were successful. But due to the economic crisis in Thailand about 35 years ago, that project did not fly and he became bankrupt, ending up with US$3 million (US$30 million present value) in debt that caused problems for all of my family members. I did not see my dad for about 10 years after that. You can imagine how an oldest son with two younger sisters could feel as he was faced with this family difficulty.

However, this incident made me a strong and responsible person. And this helped me to decide that I needed to **change** my future. I could not stay where I was in my province. My first change was to receive a better education and I decided to study very hard to get into the best high school in Bangkok: Triamudom Suksa School. Finally, after many hours of study, I was accepted into this highly-sought-after high school. Only five people from my province were invited that year.

This was like a whole new world to me; everything seemed to be different in Bangkok. Again, I needed to **change and adapt**, this time to life in a new place. The school was a far more competitive environment than I had been used to back in my province. I did well in high school and moved on to study mechanical engineering in Chulalongkorn University, the most prestigious university in the country. I graduated with honors and gained employment with Esso Thailand, an affiliate of ExxonMobil, joining a big corporation immediately after graduation. The salary was great at US$550 per month back in 1993, not a bad start for a new university graduate. I was very happy and dedicated to my work. My performance had been of the highest standard for the past 19 years, and I was promoted quickly with a high salary.

It has been a good life overall with only one exception: I found that I had less and less time for myself and my family. In 2009, at the age of 37, I started to plan for my retirement. You may think I am quite advanced for a Thai, because most Thai do not even have a retirement plan. I came to realize that even in a high position and with a large income, I could not retire young and have a life I desired. That was a wake-up call to me. I could not sleep that night and my wife asked me what was wrong? I told her we do not have a good plan for our future and she thought I was drunk. "We have a good life now," she said. "What are you talking about?" I told her I had been a good planner for my work all of my life, and so why couldn't I plan my life to create a great life after retirement as well? And my dream is, I want to retire before I am 50.

That night was the first time I had thought about changing my career to have a better life. I want a great life, not just a good life. I started to learn everything about investing, anything that could give me a better return on my money and secure my future. Before that I had never even considered any of that, simply because deep down in my subconscious mind my childhood experience about money from my dad's business failure was still haunting me. I was too fearful to take any risks, and my Mom always told me: "debt is bad," "bankers are not your friends," and things like that. Now I realized that those were my Mom's beliefs and I needed to remove them from my mind so that I could move forward with my dream. A starting point for me was to train myself and my mind through attending many world-class personal development events. These courses changed my world and my perspective about life and money forever.

The next episode of change in my life began when I decided to become involved in business and start my own company as an international consultant. I would own my life. I received a lot of resistance from my family, of course, as they deemed my business venture an unsecured path to walk. I completely understood where their thinking was coming from, and so I had to manage my way through change, challenge, and my family's resistance.

The biggest challenge, of course, was myself and whether or not I really wanted this change. Next was the people around me, especially the people who loved me. Last were others who might criticize me.

First, I had to overcome my fear and get over it, to get out of my big comfort zone. I spent a lot of time working on myself, my attitude, my dream, my goal. I believed every successful person starts with his or her thoughts. Then they create a plan and act on it. They keep on going without excuses. They are persistent and never give up.

Attitude is everything: you must have a Positive Mental Attitude, which will lead you through any change and challenge you go through. Personal development taught me the process of change:

1. Awareness
2. Understanding
3. Disassociation
4. Reprogramming

Let me tell you a little more about how I used what I learned to change my life—I think I should say, to transform my life—in just a few years.

Just to let you know, I did start my own company in 2010 despite all of the disagreements from my family. For two and a half years, I did consulting work part-time outside my regular full-time job. I quit my full-time job in 2012 after a good 19 years with a monthly income of over US$10,000. That was a very big decision for me to make. Early this year, four years after I quit my job, I accumulated my first million US dollars from my business, and I have expanded this business to many countries in the region. I now have more time with my wife and my Mom.

In fact, I am at home this morning where I'm writing this chapter after having breakfast with my Mom. My Mom is a strong lady, and this year she is 73 years old and very healthy. She is my hero. She lives with my wife and me now, and I see her every day, unlike with my previous job where I could only see her over the weekend. My priorities had shifted to spending my valuable time with my loved ones. And I have traveled extensively in the Southeast Asia region, the USA, and Europe for both business and leisure in the past few years, making more friends than I could ever have imagined.

I now own six rental properties that generate an income of over US$5,000 each month. I also have a large investment portfolio both in Thailand and in the Southeast Asia region, where I will accumulate my wealth and become financially independent without any debt within just a couple more years. Finding time to enjoy my life and my passion for traveling the world has now become a priority for my wife and me. I have decided to join the Chasing193 club and to visit every country in the world during my lifetime. According to the United Nations, there are 193 sovereign nations in the world, and I learned that there are more people who have traveled into outer space than people who have visited every country in the world. In fact, fewer than 100 people have travelled to every country in the world throughout the history of mankind. I find this ultimate travel club to be one of the most exclusive clubs on earth. They have inspired me to become one of the few people to achieve this incredible goal.

I am glad that I can pursue this because of the decision I made in 2012 to leave my safe, secure, and time-draining position. Looking back, I wonder how I managed such a dramatic life-defining change, despite all of the challenges and difficulty I had to overcome. My personal philosophy is that life begins at the end of your comfort zone.

Let's step back in time where all of this started in 2009. My regular day began something like this. The first meeting began at 6:50 a.m. because my job at the time was as an unit manager in a large oil refinery. There was an operating shift change right at 7 a.m., and, if you really wanted to know what was going on the night before, you needed to speak to the staff from the night shift. That way, I was prepared for the big management meeting at 8 a.m. I learned first-hand from various situations that it was far better for me to have the right information before I walked into that 8 a.m. meeting. This became my morning routine.

That meeting would go on and on from 8 a.m. to 10 a.m. to noon, often as a lunch meeting, to 1 p.m., 3 p.m., and right up until 5 p.m. I would then drive back to Bangkok, which is about a two-hour drive from the refinery, every day, where I would work in my start-up business and enjoy my personal interests. So, by the end of the day I probably stopped at almost midnight and I went to bed at around 1 a.m. At 4:30 a.m., I would wake up to prepare for my drive back to the refinery to be ready for my daily 6:50 a.m. meeting. What a day! I also worked Saturday and Sunday, and I had to travel to neighboring countries, like Vietnam, to meet with my business partners and clients.

It seemed liked I was always completely tired, both physically and mentally. I also faced challenges from my family as well as from my colleagues at work. One day my Mom faced me and asked why would I want to do this, as I already had a good secure job which paid very well. If you remember, my Dad's business ended in bankruptcy, and the one who suffered the most was my Mother who had three young children to take care of through a difficult financial period. For over 10 years she struggled to make ends meet. I completely understood her point of view, especially after everything she had been through.

I was aware of what had happened but understood where I was in life. I also understood that everyone has a different perspective on the same situation and circumstances. I understood that my Mom's position was born from her painful past experience about money and she did not want her child to have to go through that as well. So, for her, business was bad and risky and it's better to stay with a safe and secured job, the one I was already in. My Mom is a great lady and is very strong. She only had four years of education, but she can speak Thai, Chinese, and some basic English. She would come to me every year around the anniversary of my start date and ask how much my salary had increased over the year. And you know what? My average salary increase over the 19 years of employment had been over 15% per year.

She had a little book where she had recorded my results over those 19 years, and so she knew all about my progress at the refinery. One particular year, I received a raise of 35%. She mentioned that such an amount of increase is more than some people's full months' salaries. It's an understatement to say she was very proud of me and happy that I was in that safe and secured job. However, I had a different idea.

I listened to her, completely understanding her point of view; but, rather than argue, I asked that she give me time to prove to her that my plan was a good one. And I asked if she could trust her son, who apparently isn't stupid and would do his best in every situation to make this new dream a reality. I asked her to please support me as I am now going through a transition in life with my start-up company. I told her that if someone starts a new business it might not be an overnight success, and I am starting this part-time and keeping my full-time job for the security, and so I need time to achieve my dream. I knew she was just worried that I might have a car accident because of the danger of falling asleep while driving. I made it through the two and a half years of hardship and what I learned over that period is the Attitude of Warriors. I needed to act in spite of fear, act even when I am not in the mood, accept no excuses especially from myself, and never—Never Ever—give up on my dream.

I understand that life is a journey and I need to be open to learning new things and to constantly improve myself and to enjoy the process along the way. Two main things kept me going through this period: the single decision, and not giving up. I needed to guard my attitude; so, while driving I would always listen to personal development audios from Anthony Robbins, Jim Rohn, and T. Harv Eker. These CDs were always playing in my car.

In the two years of transition, I also attended many world-class seminars, like Anthony Robbin's Unleash the Power Within in Singapore, T. Harv Eker's Enlightened Warrior Training Camp in Malaysia, and Awareness Before Change, Goal Achievement Course & Successful Leadership Training Program (ABC/GAC/SLT). Those helped me to develop the right mindset and attitude along with my burning desire to be a success and to change my life. I also didn't want to let my Mom down. I wanted once again to show her that I can do this. I can be a leader for my family and I can control my destiny. I did this for my family, and I wanted to make my hero happy.

The two last parts of change are Disassociation and Reprogramming. I needed to get away from my past and create a completely new paradigm, or I would stay exactly the same, tied to my family's past financial failure. I needed to disassociate from that past. I started to realize that my Dad's bankruptcy had always impacted my financial decision-making process. Once I became aware of this, I began to disassociate from those thoughts and understand—with appreciation—that many of those thoughts and words were from my Mom.

Reprogramming with new information was vital to creating the life I had imagined so that I could be successful with my investments. I freed myself to move in that direction. Of course, not all of my investments were successful; I did make some mistakes and lost lots of money in my investments. But I quickly got over the failures. In the process of change, it is important that you have the ability to overcome the word "failure" and keep in mind that there is no such thing as failure, but rather a learning experience to take on board with one's future thinking. We should use any failure as a door to bigger goals. As Napoleon Hill said, "Every adversity and every failure carries with it the seed of an equal or greater benefit."

Many people ask me how I can move from being a full-time employee to becoming a successful entrepreneur with an international business and have enough assets to generate income for myself and my family and still be able to retire at a young age. What is my secret to success? I can summarize what I've learned over the past few years.

Here is my success formula:

1. Dream
2. Set Goals
3. Believe
4. Take Action
5. Lead

For me, dreaming is the first one. **DREAMs** are what gave me energy to imagine a new reality. As Michelangelo said, "The greater danger for most of us is not that our aim is too high and we miss it, but that it is too low and we reach it." So, I dream BIG because it is free to do so. I also want to be a driving force for my own life, as I believe life is a journey, and 5, 10, 20 years from now, I will reach a destination somewhere. The question is, WHERE? And what do I REALLY want out of life? I wrote all of my dreams down on a piece of paper. It started as a simple collection of thoughts. Those thoughts would later grow into many ideas, which grew into larger ideas when the details emerged.

You must have as many details as possible for your dream to become a reality. And make those dreams more visual by putting them on a board where you can see and refer to them as frequently as possible. In this process, you must find your WHY, which will be your driving force toward that dream. The more powerful your WHY, the more powerful your commitment.

I also have a dream to be able to travel the world. I think this started when I was 24 and was still a young engineer. One day my company announced an education assistant program for full-time students to study abroad. I immediately applied for this program. The only problem was, as a Thai graduate, I could barely speak English, and the company only accepted employees who could do so. The educational program was to study in one of the top 10 Universities in the USA.

My heart was beating fast when I had this dream. I then started to study hard on my English. Luckily, I had my best American boss, Kary Saleeby, who supported me in this endeavor. He forced me to use English daily at work and to write in English as well. This helped me to be able to earn a good English score on my standardized test, and I was finally accepted to Duke University, University of Texas at Austin, and Cornell University. I decided to go to Engineering College at Cornell University in Ithaca, New York, and that was the start of my world exploration.

The USA was the first long-distance international travel that I was to experience. I still remember my big boss calling me into his office for the orientation before departing, and he told me that my job was not to be great at academics but to see the world. I did just that, visiting a total of 35 states in the US during that two-year period, as well as most of the national parks on the West Coast. And I became president of the Cornell Thai Association when we first launched the Thai Festival as part of the Southeast Asia Cultural Week. My dream stayed with me throughout my stay in the U.S. However, when I resumed my work life again in Thailand, I just didn't have enough time to further pursue my dream of visiting every country. Now, a few years after I started my own business, I will begin again to chase my dream of visiting every **country in the world!**

I SET GOALS to be able to retire before reaching the age of 50, and I expected to succeed. I had decided to win this goal and began with the end in mind. The word "decision" comes from the same Latin root as "incision," and means "to cut off from." So, when you make a 100% decision it means you cut off any other alternative. Set goals that will lead you in the direction towards your dream and put a timeline to it. I looked at my financial portfolio and worked out how much money I would need after 50 to live the lifestyle I desired. I needed to find a way to get more income and make the most of my investments. I focused on assets that produced a recurring income like rental properties, share dividends, and business. Then my mind started to work with razor focus and determination. I also believed that, if you want something badly, you will signal that to the universe and the universe will respond in your favor. There are no coincidences in life; everything happens for a reason and that reason is to support me with my dream.

Thought is energy; it can transmit without media. It will help you to meet the right people who can help you or mentor you or to find the right business partner or the right business opportunities.

This is exactly what happened on my journey, from acquiring the right property that gave me both capital gains and great rental returns, to the right long-term stocks to invest in, to the right partners in my business in the region. I know I attracted all these scenarios into my life. I also set personal goals to visit at least one new country a year. Travelling will always be a strong passion in my life. Many of my friends think that I'm crazy to have such large goals. However, I think that if no one is laughing at your goals, it means your goals aren't big enough.

One time my wife and I went to Japan on our way to Hawaii. It was not the first time we had visited Japan, but it was just different this time around. We didn't have any concrete plans and we didn't rush around to see everything. We just planned as we went along. Every morning I asked my wife where she wanted to go that day. Then we went there at a slow, gentle pace. No permission to go on leave from work, no preset schedule, no early wake-up call in the morning, and no rushing around. If we wanted to enjoy coffee in a nice café that we passed by, we did and stayed as long as we liked. I loved it. I felt FREEDOM for the first time, and that was what had been my driving force towards achieving my goals. Not just money. I wanted time and someone to enjoy this with me as well.

You will meet many critics along your journey as you set big goals and as you push yourself to reach them. When you are dealing with change, you need to turn to your supporters and ignore your critics. Critics could be well-meaning people, but they place fear in your way. Please recognize these fears as simply misplaced concerns. Don't let these fears sway you from your path. Find and align with people who are your true friends, and they will support you in positive ways. Stay away from negative people. That's the best advice I can give you.

Another hard part of my journey was to **BELIEVE**. Believe in myself; embrace What Will Be; believe that I can do it. Self-belief is like a muscle: I needed to practice believing that everything would work out for the best and keep building on my belief. I set off to meet with successful people in my field and learned as much as I could from them. I found and worked with many role models and duplicated what they had done to achieve their successes. I learned their attitudes, their mindsets, even how they dressed and spoke. Magically, this worked for me, too, because I believe success is a science. Find someone who did it before you and learn from them. Have you ever heard the term "Fake it till you make it"? Or the saying "Be, Do, Have"? Act like the person you want to be and do what they do; then you're going to have what they have. Trust me, it works! Ask me anything you want to know about what I do and how I do. If I can be of any help to you, trust me I will.

I've often noticed many people who have walked the same road as me but have become defeated. I myself have also faced many challenges and setbacks, but I viewed them as merely challenges to overcome. I did this not just for myself but for my loved ones as well. I also knew that whatever I thought about—positive or negative—I would eventually believe. So, I only focused on positive thoughts, and I kept finding evidence in my world that my belief is accurate and possible.

'Change'

Every time I encounter a setback, I always ask myself these two questions: What can I learn from this? What will I do better next time? There are a lot of people who overcome obstacles and create successful outcomes. Nothing is impossible. All of these people dare to Dream, Set Goals, and Believe. I am still working on my inner game in regard to this. To achieve positive results, you must do something about the thing you focus on and think about.

This leads to the next point and some most necessary steps towards success: **TAKE ACTION**! I should say, TAKE MASSIVE ACTION! Not just any action. And the action must take you in the direction which aligns with your dreams and goals. I've seen many people do busy work or wait until the perfect moment to take action, and this is a mistake. There is no such thing as perfect. The number one difference between those who achieve success and those who do not is ACTION. Action is the only bridge between your inner world and your outer world or between dream and reality. You can have all of the belief and skills in the world, but without focused action nothing will come to realization.

This is what I did best. I am a person of action; I am very focused, and I keep on going until I achieve my desired result. As my boss always said, if there is a situation with pressure, put me in the thick of it and I will kick ass. That's me. One of my main strengths is working better under pressure. Taking action requires a belief in yourself and your dream. You need to believe in your dream before you see it. Once you have that belief, then you must act.

It's normal to have some doubt, too, but don't let that doubt stop you in the pursuit of your dream. Henry Ford once said, "Whether you think you can or can't, you're right." The power of your positive thoughts can help you on your journey to success. So, you need to reverse any negative thoughts, whether they come from you or someone else. Silence the critics. Keep telling yourself you can do it and take focused action in the right direction to turn your dreams into reality. You will need your strong purpose or your strong WHY to motivate you to act and to keep going when things become tough.

The last of my steps in this success formula is **LEAD**. When I first began my career in the oil refinery, one of my senior managers asked me how I will know when I'm ready to progress to the next level in leadership? I didn't really know the answer. He told me, "When you can handle your boss's job, then you are ready." He told me that again before he gave me his job.

I saw people getting hired because of their professional abilities, but they didn't progress to the next level because they didn't know how to lead others. I saw people move ahead that weren't as talented or educated as others, but they had vision, drive, and the ability to lead people. The more you can lead others, the higher position you will receive, and the higher the pay you will receive as well. I would also like to add that the more people you serve, the better leader you become!

Leaders follow leaders; so, I will first be a good follower and grow as I move into becoming a leader. Success in life will come as a result of continually learning and growing. Consequently, my primary goal is to learn to be a good leader by following great leaders and replicating their success. This requires you to get out of your comfort zone in search of growth. In life, no one achieves success solely on their own. Every successful person has had associates, friends, family members, or someone who contributed to their success. Life is truly a team sport, both in work and in one's personal life.

Once you help others to create value, your contribution will not go unnoticed. Here is testimony to this. One day, I received a call and learned that I was appointed to be on the External Board of Directors and Auditing Committee for one of the largest publicly traded companies in the Thai stock market. This company is also a market leader in its field.

'Change'

I was a bit surprised as to why they chose me. Most of the time, board directors in Thailand are people who are much more senior and somewhere near retirement age. I asked the board why, and the answer I received was because of my valuable experiences and knowledge in my career of almost 20 years in the oil refinery. They also said my enthusiasm is second to none and I have an attitude of always striving to contribute, which is hard to find in the market at the moment.

I never knew such an opportunity existed, and it would mean stepping outside my comfort zone. I took on the challenge and, in less than two years, that company changed their business model. They began to profit again after 10 years of declining revenue, and the company stock went up significantly. I contributed a lot to the bottom line, increasing the value of the business to the shareholders.

I used the success formula I shared with you and moved myself along in this wonderful journey we call life. I am glad there are so many amazing people in my life: all of my friends, my family, my Dad Decho, my Mom Sirirak, my wife Umaporn, all of my mentors, my clients, my business partners. I am grateful they are in my life, and I have a lot of gratitude for everything they have done for me. I'm grateful for everything that has happened in my life, because I believe everything happens for a reason. However, nothing has a meaning except for the meaning we give it. We are responsible for our lives. While I truly believe that change is inevitable, I have total control over my future and the meaning I give it. Socrates is famous for saying, "The Secret of Change is to focus all of your energy, not on fighting the old, but on building the new." Everything is impermanent; thus, the only thing that is certain is change. Embrace it, love it, and enjoy your journey.

Chapter 6
Living With Change

By Pavel Helstyn

I dedicate my chapter to my mother, Marie Helstynova, who always took everything upon herself and endured so much only to always make us feel safe. A debt I can never repay. The most humble and selfless person I have ever known.

It is a fail

Everybody feels like a failure sometimes, despite what we see on social media, TV, or anywhere else. And there is a simple reason for that. It is the truth.

You will fail and you will feel like a failure. Yes, you will. If you are reading this, you already have. I certainly have many times and will continue to do so.

Today is one of those days. A bad day. As I wake up this morning at 4 a.m., I wake to a particularly bad feeling. I'm not an early riser; I just could not sleep tonight. I went to bed just after midnight, but I woke up again at 1, then at 2, then at 3. And at 4, I'm just done trying. I am sick to my stomach, and I'm coming down with something. The last few days have been tough on my mind. It feels like I'm spinning in circles.

I'm leaving Barcelona, the city I love, in two days. I have to because my finances do not allow me to stay any longer. If something does not happen rather quickly, my business will go bankrupt in a month. As a cherry on the top of the cake, a tenant in my apartment 1000 miles away has not paid rent in two months and has stopped communicating. And, since I broke up with my girlfriend a few months ago, I have not been able to make a real connection with another woman.

I am a little scared, and slight panic is creeping in every time I think about all of this.

If you are reading this, chances are good that you like to read books on success. Success is very important to all of us, and so we like to read about it. We like to think about it. I am the same. However, my problem is this: most books are only written about success. We don't hear about hard times much anymore.

Most success authors will tell you that they went through hard times a long time ago. They will tell you how they fantastically overcame all obstacles and you can too if you follow their success principles. Still, if you are like me, you cannot shake the feeling that they are enormously successful and that's how they have been their whole life. It might not be true, but that's how it feels. It feels like stars have aligned for them. It feels like you just cannot connect. It all feels too distant.

We naturally believe what we see at the moment and what we are experiencing. For the human mind, it is extremely difficult to acknowledge and deeply believe in progress and the hard work that went into it. We see and live in the now, on the surface. Based on what I have written so far, you might have realized that I am feeling like a failure right now, and you are quite right. But am I a failure? Am I ready to jump off a cliff, or do I feel like the world is about to end? Absolutely not. I deeply believe that everything is all right. That's what my story is about. It is about being in the middle of a storm and getting out. If you ever find yourself in the middle of a storm as well, there might be something for you here.

The bad in all the Good

Since I can remember, I have always been interested in personal development and making the best of one's life. I never really felt like I had enough experience to share that would offer anything valuable to those that need it, though. When John asked me to contribute to this book, I was a little skeptical at first, but, as I thought about it, I came to believe there might be something I could add.

I love watching videos and reading advice from Tony Robbins and other great mentors. It fires me up, it helps me to expand my horizons, and it generally moves me forward. However, there are two things that I usually miss. First, I find it difficult to identify with enormously successful people. I admire them and wish them all the success and wealth and health they have, and I aspire to reach their level of happiness. I believe they show us the way. But from where I am right now, it is simply too much of a gap to close. It is a subconscious thing that I am aware of. Second, I feel not enough attention is paid to negatives and bad times. If they are mentioned, they are usually way back in the past. All in all, this makes it all the more difficult to believe these successful people are not super humans rather than normal people like you and me.

I am not mentioning the negatives to bring you down or because I want to complain or because I want you to save me. It is simply that I am being honest with myself. In person, I will probably tell you all of this with a smile on my face.

If, at this point, you think I am crazy, let me tell you why I think I am not. I see life the way I live it, as a bunch of dots: actions, feelings, moments, encounters. As I look back, these dots become lines. Some dots never connect; some do. Some of those that connect will meet along the same path. Where the most dots connect on the path, that is where I find my lifeline. As I look back at some of my life experiences, there are dots that repeat themselves. These are repeating emotions, actions, and concepts that shape me and eventually take me where I am.

These repeating dots are my principles. They have momentum. They are more powerful than any random negative feeling or action at any moment. They run through everything. Every time I apply them, they have a very similar effect on my life. I believe anyone can use them when dealing with difficulties and changes, expected or not. Over the years, these concepts have constantly helped me to get through an entire spectrum of difficulties in life. And every time I have mistreated these principles, I have found myself in trouble.

Having thought about this, I realized that this is what I want to share—my life as a regular person and my guiding principles. Maybe you will find a piece of your normality in my normality and my slightly negative story. Maybe it will help you to acknowledge your pain today, calm down, start building your momentum, and move forward. If there is one person who does, I am happy. That, I hope, can be my contribution.

What follows is an account of three of my life-changing events on the background of me growing as a person and my principles as I have discovered them.

Managing Trauma

We are often told that we are the rulers of our destiny; whatever we want, we can achieve, control, and change. Sometimes life puts us in a situation that makes us question these ideas and leaves us hopeless. We go through trauma. The emotional earthquake is so strong that it makes us question everything. We become passengers instead of the drivers of our lives.

When I was 17, I lost my father, a change so major that I became a bystander in my own life for many years. Taking back the driver's seat was a very gradual process for me. It taught me some of the most important lessons in life. This is how it happened, on the background of what shaped me as a person growing up and what I learned in the process.

How It Started

I had never really thought about it much, but change has influenced my life and the lives of everyone around me tremendously. Things that happened shaped the people around me, where they went in life, and the views they adopted to the point that, looking back, some of it seems almost like a movie.

I was born into completely different times from what we have today. I was born into communist Czechoslovakia. Things were not so good back then. I don't remember much about it, as I was six when the revolution came in 1989 and my country adopted democracy, but there are quite a few things that I do remember. Also, without our knowing it at the time, the revolution in my country started a chain of events that would have a seismic effect on me and my whole family.

I was born into what you would call a perfect family. I had an older sister, and our parents loved us both very much. They were university sweethearts, and they were the type of couple that did everything together. They were perfectly aligned in opinions at home and in the type of household they should provide for us as we were growing up. Except when we misbehaved, they never let us worry about anything. We were raised with values such as respect, understanding, and honesty.

Being a kid in communist Czechoslovakia in the 1980s meant a few things to me. Buying stuff was extremely difficult. Watermelons, which I loved, were only available during about a three-week period each year. Store shelves were usually half-filled or completely empty, and shop assistants were almost universally very grumpy. The most pervasive feelings in society were feelings of mistrust, hopelessness, and general fear. These are things I just observed but did not understand then and would come to realize only many years later as an adult.

There were certain things that we were simply not allowed to talk about, and there was only so much that our parents shared with us, as they tried to protect us and our family from crossing the party line. No one knew which neighbor was an STB[1] agent, and that was a worry. An STB agent was a type of a secret agent, often recruited from the general public, whose main purpose was to report to authorities any ideological deviations of neighbors, friends, and even family. The fear to speak was omnipresent, and my sister and I were often told not to talk about something in public. But in the mind of a six-year-old, this did not bother me much. I thought it was normal. My biggest problems were the horrible food we were getting served in the school canteen and being forced to finish it, being on time to school with my girlfriend, and playing soccer (football) in the park afterwards. There were no computers or mobile phones, and there was zero traffic on our street although we lived in the city center. So, my friends and I just hung out outdoors all the time. Our television was black and white with no remote. It ran two state channels. My personal pinnacle of technology was a wind-up watch that I was required to wear when I went out. Any other time, it was neatly put away in the drawer so as not to come to any harm.

Both of my parents were university educated and worked in state-owned companies. There was no free enterprise back then. My dad worked as an economic deputy at the biggest wholesale/retail shoe company in Czechoslovakia, and my mom worked as a clerk. At that time, everything was set from the moment you were born until the moment you die. The government controlled most things, including all of the prices and the stuff we could buy, the countries we could travel to, the jobs, the salaries, the things we could say, and the information we were getting through state-owned media.

---

1 STB stands for Státní bezpečnost which translates literally as State Security.

Then, on November 17, 1989, as in many other countries of the Eastern Bloc, the people of Czechoslovakia, led by students, decided to put an early end to the 20th century and start a new era for our land. I remember going to the local square with my parents. It was packed so tightly that you could not move. The coolest thing to me was that my dad let me sit on his shoulders so that I was above what seemed to be one hell of a party. I was in first grade back then and we were required to call teachers "comrade teacher." Everybody at the square was cheerful and happy and full of hope. Unknowingly, as well, everybody was as unprepared as it gets for what was to come. Little did I know that this was the beginning of life as a continuous lesson. In expectation of freedom and democracy, this was probably the most unforeseen reality by most people. Change was about to hit us like a bus at 60 miles per hour.

November 17, 1989, was one dot on my lifeline that was planted like a seed then and there, and 12 years later it would catch up with me and my whole family at full force.

It is very common that people will focus on major events, but such events are almost universally a result of something that creeps in and builds up over time. As a little boy, I did not understand this. Looking back now, I see the things that were happening went in sequence and in an obvious pattern. Patterns are in everything we do. It is as straightforward as exercise. Regular exercise gives you a strong body and a sharp mind. Heavy drinking and overeating makes your life go to ruin. Connecting the dots will eventually result in a major event, one we would often call life changing. But these life-changing events usually start a long time before we realize what has happened. Few understood this back then, as communism had never put them in a position to ponder such things. It was all the less obvious to me, an oblivious six-year-old.

Without my realizing it, the ascent of my country to democracy would mean the beginning of the longest never-ending lesson I would ever have in understanding patience and persistence, two main principles that I always look back to when feeling weak and tired.

Misunderstanding Opportunity

Two generations—more than 41 years—were lost to our social experiment with communism. That is where my parents grew up. They were 36 years old when the revolution came.

When everything that we know, no matter how unpleasant, disappears from under our feet and we are thrown into the dark, it is something unimaginable to most of us. Similar to a prisoner released after decades in prison, we did not know how to deal with our newly acquired freedom. What followed were years that signified major changes in our society. This was sometimes referred to as the Wild East.

As the young democracy and market economy slowly went through reforms and got on its feet, many paid an individual price for the better future of our nation. For the first time in their lives, people experienced losing jobs for reasons other than the ideological reasons they had known before. They were presented with the idea of competition, and our savings-oriented economy slowly changed into a consumer economy. Companies started being massively privatized in a process in which some made billions and some lost their life's savings and careers and were, for the first time, thrown into the job market having to show their skills, negotiate their salaries, and look for opportunities. This was a completely new concept.

Dealing with change became the central theme of the young democracy and this affected the lives of everyone. Some adapted and some got caught in the middle, stuck with the old views of entitlement and misunderstanding the new dynamic. I did not pay much attention to the bigger picture at the time. I was just a kid growing up, trying to deal with my own growing up issues. Even though all of these seismic changes were something that I could hardly influence, they shaped my life for the next 12 years in one way and then for the next 16 years in another. All of these years have been a lesson that lasts to this day.

Only Way Forward

In 2001, I was about to turn 18. I was learning to drive so that I could get my license, and life was kind of happening. On the 24th of March, my Mom and I were returning from a weekend visit with my grandparents. I remember this day very well. It was the first time that my Mom had let me drive her car. I had always been a car enthusiast, something I shared with my Dad. This was a big deal for me. I was looking forward to coming back home and telling everyone. As we pulled up to our apartment building, I immediately noticed something was wrong. It was hard to tell what, but it was. The front door was wide open. There was a big strange-looking black car outside. Our apartment windows were wide open as well, and I started to get the feeling that this had something to do with us. I was completely at odds with what it could be, however. The black car was a hearse. As I relive this moment, it still draws tears to my eyes.

As we parked the car, my sister rushed out of the building crying. Dad had hung himself.

I could not understand what was going on. I was in shock, but I was also completely empty and confused at the same time. My relationship with my dad had been problematic because he had been an alcoholic for the last few years and he'd constantly fought with my mother. He almost never talked to us, either out of shame or because he was out drinking. But he was still my dad who had taught me so much, and I loved him. That day, I did not know what to feel, and, all the more, I didn't know what to do.

After that, I don't remember much of what happened. I only remember bits and pieces of what followed. The following year, I was about to graduate from high school. I remember almost nothing about that year except that I was rarely ever there. More coherent memories came back somewhere around graduation and later as I enrolled in university.

My life was never the same after my dad's death. I do understand how general this sounds, but that is the only way I can put it.

I remember those early days especially by the range of emotions I felt. First and most immediate was emptiness. That was the first time I had discovered how big of a part some people play in our lives, even if we do not comprehend it while they are with us. When they are suddenly gone, it is like a piece of us is torn out, leaving nothing, just an empty space that you need to fill over time. I got stuck on "What? How? What? Why? How? Why? What?" and repeat. Over and over again. There were no answers, only questions. Then emptiness.

Then, after a while, emptiness changed into anger. That is when those questions expanded into "What the hell? Why would anyone do this? Why would you do this to us?" The intensity of this slowly phased out, but it took several years to completely come to terms with the situation.

Emptiness and anger were the most immediate and obvious emotions that I could name. They came along with confusion, sadness, fear, and a few others. But judging from a distance, these were not the most life altering emotions; they were simply the most immediate and intense in the moment. What changed my life the most was what was created beneath those emotions, beneath the surface.

The emotions combined with the experience were like ingredients formed into a recipe of who I am and who I was as a person. There were a few patterns that I unconsciously adopted.

First, I developed almost complete emotional numbness to protect myself from pain. Consequently, I found it extremely difficult to enjoy anything. As my ability to be hurt was suspended, so was my ability to find happiness. It seems that pain defines happiness. In the long term, you cannot avoid one without losing the other. For a while, I lost both. Connected with this was another capability I adopted: to give up anything anytime. "Whatever" and "it does not matter" became the words to express the ultimate motto of my life. This was partially connected with the numbness and partially with the role model I'd known in life. When you see the person who gave you life give up his own, it makes you think that giving up is always an option. And since you do not care about much of anything, you accept it as the norm. And so I did.

As you can imagine, my level of alienation from society gradually grew. This was demonstrated by my hobbies and in my relationships with the people around me, as well as in anything I would or would not want to do. It made my student years rather solitary and caused me to partially miss out on a bunch of interesting things in my early 20s. I just did not care. Or so I thought.

My only luck was that my mother had taught me a strong sense of discipline. I am very grateful to her for this, because, among other things, it eventually put me through university. If it were up to me only, I would have given up. She had a harder time than my sister and me. She had to look after us. And she never complained or gave up. It was a lot to live up to. Her example somehow led me forward. Thanks to her, I felt the responsibility to keep moving on without even knowing it at the time.

Nonetheless, my emotional numbness and careless attitude sabotaged me for many years. This could happen because I did not know these obstacles were there, which made dealing with them quite difficult. All the time, I thought I was doing the right thing, and these guards kept me in my safe bubble. Funny enough, I did not think I had a problem. I thought that my solution of hiding away was perfectly functional. For a while it was and it was comfortable.

In my family, we never talked about my dad's passing—what preceded it and what it caused. I owe much to my friend, Petr Stryk, for opening me up. He helped me to discover that not talking about something important with someone you care for, in effect, equals lying. It will hurt you as a person. Not talking kept me in my bubble and prevented me from accepting reality. As with everything, when I refused to accept reality in one area, it spilled over into many others.

As we talked, Petr and I gradually gained each other's trust. This gave me a feeling of safety. By not feeling judged, I could again start to rediscover my deeper emotions about life, especially the negative ones. Instead of pushing my bad feelings away by saying whatever, I started exploring them, discovering where they came from and what they caused. As I discovered what bothered me, I also started learning about what mattered to me once again.

I learned how important it is to look after the family that you bring into this world, how important you are to them and how important it is to care and to have people around that support you. I learned the responsibility each of us has. By quitting, you are not only quitting on yourself; you are quitting on the generations before you and the generations after you. You are quitting on the people around you who care. You are quitting on those that did not quit on you.

I also learned how to better deal with the truth itself. Not only the convenient truth, but also the relevant, real one and why it matters. I learned how important it is to get out of emotional comfort zones, to live life with all of its ups and downs and to accept it. Accepting it makes you a better, wiser, more open person. Shying away makes you weaker, closed, and sad. It makes you drift along, never aspiring for anything in life because you do not know what you like. If you cannot define what you like, you cannot get it. That is a sad path to be on.

Most importantly, this taught me about the value and healing power of time. As much as I would have liked to have been able to deal with everything right away, the truth is, it took time. It took finding the right people around me, asking questions, and discovering weaknesses and then facing them. It required acknowledging that I cared when I failed at something. It took accepting that my feelings got hurt, but that it is ok; getting hurt is a part of the quest for happiness. As I started to open up to what I did not like and learned to live through the emotions, in turn, I gained positive emotions.

This process has never stopped, and I know it will continue into the future. That is the important role of time and patience. We have to learn that growing, i.e. dealing with change, is a continual, often painful, process. There is never the one right answer that will solve all problems. As we face hardships, patience and perseverance are key.

We can often feel under pressure to deal with everything immediately. Solving is everything. It's the pressure of perfection—the aspiration to achieve—that makes us think we have to be able to tick off all the boxes. It makes us think that we are always in control. To a certain extent, yes, but in my case, focusing on the journey rather on the goal was much more important in dealing with my trauma and finding happiness.

If you do not have patience and focus on the journey, it is easy to get disappointed. It is easy to give up if you do not reach what you want quickly. Patience in trying is key. As you try, new ways will uncover and new opportunities will appear. As you keep trying continuously, more and more richness and happiness will find a way into your life.

Talking in great detail about my dad's suicide will probably never be something I am totally at ease with. It feels too personal. But, through my healing process, I discovered it is not something that should be hidden from others. That hurts everyone. It is a part of stepping out of my comfort zone that needs to be done, although instinct tells one otherwise. It took me a long time to understand this. I believe I am not the only one who feels this way, and that is why I decided to put it in this book. I hope I can ease the healing process for someone else who is reading this.

The two following sections are a lot more active in discussing how change can be approached, and I put a lot more emphasis on things we can affect. I feel, however, that the previous section was important as it helps us, through patience and acceptance, to deal with things we cannot easily influence.

Resisting Change

Sometimes you find yourself in a situation where you get a little stuck, sometimes even without your conscious awareness. There will be a nagging feeling at the back of your mind telling you something should change, but the action will be missing.

Probably the biggest planned change in my life so far has been the decision to quit my job and become an entrepreneur. Despite all that was happening to me emotionally, I remember this was something I had thought about since I was in my early 20s. And even though I feel like everybody is an entrepreneur these days, true or not, I certainly did not feel that way back then. The decision was all the more difficult for me because I had a very prestigious, high-paying job. It took me a long time to make my decision and then act on it in a big way.

About a year and a half after finishing university, I entered the world of management consulting. I started working for a division of an international IT company that specialized in deploying data based risk management and marketing processes in multinational banks. It was a hell of a challenge. Dealing with experienced managers and board members of large corporations was a new and slightly intimidating thing for me as a 27-year-old. The travel schedule was unrelenting, requiring us to travel almost every week leaving Sunday night and coming back home Friday night. We had less than 48 hours of down time with families, girlfriends, etc. It sometimes drove me crazy, and we did have disagreements at work just like anywhere else, but I loved the job. It was the ultimate challenge. It put my mind to work. If I ever have to go back to employment, this is the kind of job I would go back to.

No matter how amazing this job was, however, I had always felt that entrepreneurial bug. It had always been something blurry on the horizon—a dream that I had hoped would materialize one day. But that is all it was: just a dream, not a goal. Internally, I did not believe it could happen. I just felt it might be nice if it could happen. It would be a journey that would take me several years to begin. I eventually did, and to this day it is the best thing that I have ever done. This journey has helped me to better understand who I really am, to improve my relationships, and to develop most as a person.

But getting there was not easy. It was a perfect example of resisting a change that I subconsciously wanted and needed.

Looking back, I can identify three key stages that I went through. Now, every time I am faced with a change that I internally feel is necessary, I go through this process.

1st Key: The Gut

Everything starts with the instinct. If I get the feeling something is not right or something should change, most often it is correct. I never see the results upfront, but I trust the instinct. Although I felt I had a great job, I also felt that something in my life was missing. At the time, I attributed this to the job itself and it brought me all the way to thinking that the job was not good. That was by no means true, though. The reality was that I felt I was not getting what I wanted. It was just the shortcut my mind took to understand that I did not like what I had. I was blaming circumstances for not getting what I wanted without even realizing it. And, as usual, there was a hint of my hidden family issues that I mentioned in the previous section.

I constantly felt I was missing out on a great adventure, one that I could define myself. I bathed in the feeling of general internal anger over the inability to take action. I had no idea what kind of action I should take, what I should do, or how I should do it. It was just my gut that told me that something should change. At that point, I decided to do one thing. I decided to start expressing these feelings openly, first to myself and then to those around me. I talked to my friends about the need for change, and I talked to myself as well.

I had no idea of what the change should be. I just acknowledged the fact it would need to happen. It may sound very simple, but sometimes we find ourselves on the beaten paths and it is very hard to think outside the box. We are so focused on getting right what we are already doing that we forget there are alternatives. This used to happen to me a lot. In time, I discovered that I can control change in my life much better by letting go of my ego and acknowledging the fact that change is an option. Once I did, opportunities started popping up.

This simple fact, applied in different scenarios, helped me to discover Southeast Asia, to redefine myself in Barcelona, and to start a business that makes everything else in my life possible.

2nd Key: Escape vs Elimination and Focus

I am an analytical person and there is one strategy that I adopted a long while ago. It helped me in this case as well. This was to put things in the simplest terms. It would sound something like this: Do not focus on what you want to abandon, but identify your ideal and go towards it.

This concept took me a long time to discover and to put to work. I see a lot of my friends make the same mistake when thinking about changing something, whether in their personal lives or in their professional lives. We tend to focus on running away from something bad, such as a bad partner, a bad job, or a bad situation.

We all know that the idea of running away from something sounds immature. It was hardwired into my brain that running away should not be done. I was taught to face problems, not to run away from them. The real questions were different for me, though: How do you make change happen when you do not run away from something? Is not change the embodiment of running away?

How do you know when it is the right time to change and when not to change? What is the point at which you should change your circumstances: the job, the partner, or something else? This bothered me until I discovered a better question. Tony Robbins says it well: If you want better answers, start asking better questions.

The immediate reflex that comes from having a gut feeling and discovering a need to change something is to think about what should be eliminated. It is a natural shortcut our brain seeks when it has to look for solutions that it already knows. The easiest and quickest thing to do is to quit. This is something that a brain can easily grasp and—voilà!—problem solved. What a halfbaked solution!

If you want good results, the right question to ask is not "Should I quit?" or "Should I leave?" but "What is it that I don't like here?" More importantly, one should ask, "What do I want instead?" Running away from something should not be an end goal in and of itself. However, if it is a part of running towards something, it becomes a necessity. Once I started asking myself the right questions, it did not take long until I discovered a few things that were very important to me which I had not been getting. I wanted to manage my own time, make independent decisions about who I talk to, where I go and when, and to have a direct relationship between the effort that I put into work and the reward I get.

Leaving something will most likely not make you happy in its own right. Defining what you want and then achieving it will bring long-term joy and a sense of accomplishment, which directly translates into happiness and healthy self-esteem. This explains the difference between escape, something undesirable, versus elimination and focus, something essential. When I discovered this, leaving my job became part of something bigger, more important, more complex. It became inevitable and necessary, and it also shrunk in importance. From the end goal, leaving that job suddenly became only a milestone. It turned from negative to positive.

These days, when I get that gut feeling, I always focus on that which I am looking towards, and that defines what I will have to leave behind.

3rd Key: Name Your Mental Roadblocks/Anchors

Once I defined what I wanted, a whole new universe opened in front of me. I suddenly had an idea of where I was going. I wanted to become a location-independent entrepreneur, to be able to work and live anywhere I might choose.

Interestingly, at this point, I still did not feel ready enough to take action. Yes, it is great to give your dream some shape, but there are usually a bunch of factors that determine where you are, and they keep you in place. Unless you pay close attention to those factors, they will generally demonstrate themselves in very simple terms. You will tell yourself that you cannot do it, which is usually just another way of saying that you are afraid. That is what I secretly told myself. The dream was just too big.

We are often told we just need to set a direction and take action. This might be true for simple things, like starting to go to the gym, buying something you can afford, or inviting friends over for dinner, things where there are little to no roadblocks and you generally know how to do it. However, with more complex and sometimes life-altering decisions, I find this advice to be grossly insufficient. I find there is a layer of factors—mental roadblocks—that keep you from actually taking action. They blur your vision and do not allow you to see the end goal. To take action, you need to eliminate those roadblocks. It usually boils down to one or two main reservations. Discovering them is the hard part. In my case, the determining factor was finance. In retrospect, it all seems clear and easy, but, at the time, it was just a cloud of questions and insecurities that needed to be cleared away.

I had defined what I wanted, but I did not know how to accomplish it. I could not even imagine what it would be like. Sitting in an office in a suit selling my time for money was the only thing I knew. (I know how this sounds, but, in essence, that is what it was.) I could not imagine any other way, let alone being able to lie on the beach somewhere in Asia, not answering to anybody. So, with the aid of self-help books and podcasts, I embarked on a journey of discovery that would take several months and, to a certain extent, still lasts until today. I started naming my fears. I discovered for myself a common psychological fact: only after you name your fear can you start to fight it. Otherwise you do not know what you are fighting. You cannot hit something you do not take aim at.

Through self-doubt, fear of the unknown (which I would learn to manage later and talk about it in the next section), and a bunch of other factors, it all came down to a very simple and almost mundane problem I already mentioned: the ability to support myself; i.e., money. Immediately, the solution became much easier and everything else became kind of secondary.

To be completely honest, I could not foresee all of the other things I would lose by leaving my job, such as personal connections, but money seemed like the biggest roadblock. As soon as this came to light, it was just a matter of mathematics. I quantified a qualitative problem. How much did I need per month, how much did I have saved, and how ready was I to start generating income ASAP? It turned out that renting out my apartment online on AirBNB was quite a nice way to add a few dollars to my bottom line while my savings lasted. This added some income for a few months and made me feel comfortable enough to say that I should give it a try. So, I did that. It was all this simple after all. I had a good road plan that I could follow, and so I gave it a shot.

Naming my roadblocks, my fears, and quantifying them was the key to giving my change momentum. It took over a year before I was faced with another change, one for which I would have no answers and no way to come up with answers. I would be completely at a loss. I came near my first bankruptcy.

Managing the Unknown (bankruptcy time)

I believe that the term bankruptcy is incorrectly coined and misunderstood. It is understood as an end to something. Almost like death. It is the result of de-humanizing life. I believe the only real bankruptcy is death. That is when you lose all of your assets. Everything else is just temporarily running out of cash. It does not matter whether you go through legal proceedings or not. It is still just a lack of cash. While you have your life and abilities, you still have the biggest assets in the game. I have gone through this three times. The first one was the scariest, as I was one week from having no money for food.

We have a saying in my mother tongue that goes along the lines of "Money will be there and we won't." The general idea behind it is this: Do not worry about money so much. It is larger than you and you cannot control it. Look out for yourself first; money is just a tool. Whatever you do, it will go its own way.

No matter how clever this sounds, being in a situation when you are temporarily out of cash, or bankrupt, you have no secure job, your business is not going well, and if this is something that happens to you for the first time before you are even making any good money, it is probably the scariest thing that you have ever been through. The second time and third time is not as bad. But the first time, it is scary and it hurts.

It hurts for several reasons. It hurts your ego. You think you amount to nothing and your ideals for a bright future get crushed. You feel like a failure in front of your friends and family. In my case, I stopped talking to a lot of them because I was so ashamed. Now I know what a bad idea this was and I have not repeated this mistake since. Aside from these ego-adjusting effects that, in reality, turned out to be very healthy for me, there were two other factors that made it so difficult. First was the element of the unknown. The first time this happened to me, I let my emotions take over and run lose. I almost completely lost my mind and only thought about the end. I kept repeating to myself that it was over. I was in it alone, ashamed to talk to anyone and completely relieved of any logical thinking that would guide me through the situation. I was running purely on instinct.

The second element that made it one of the scariest experiences of my life was that it was sustained. It was this fear that was always at the back of my mind. I would wake up in the morning and feel it. Any interaction I had throughout the days with anyone mirrored these feelings of me as upcoming failure, not knowing what to do. I went to sleep with the same feeling knowing that tomorrow would be one step closer to the end.

Surprisingly, looking back, this ended up being the most life-changing, satisfying, strength-inducing, and self-discovering experience of my life. It pushed me beyond limits and helped me to find new ones. It prepared me better than any class, book, or motivational speech for any problems that I encounter these days, and it also taught me that sometimes—very often—you just have to believe. Believe that there is a better day. Believe that you will somehow make it. The only other alternative is death, which waits for everyone, no matter what. So, there is no need to panic really.

I do not want to leave this on a completely esoteric note, however. Belief in yourself is not something intangible. Quite the contrary. Belief in yourself means working hard every day. Belief in yourself is switching to your instincts when all emotions fail you and focusing on that which is important. When you do not know what to do and have no way to find out, belief in yourself is saying, this is what I will do. Belief in yourself is not lying in bed and giving in and hoping. Belief in yourself is getting up and trying. Belief in yourself must be helped along!

And that is what I did. I had a strategy I followed and I did not stop. I wish I could say that I am a natural born leader and that I did not give up and kept fighting and I knew what to do. I cannot. More than that, I was scared to death that I could not stop and I had absolutely no idea if anything I did would be at all useful. But, at this point, something in my brain changed. Instead of doing what I wanted, something inside let me do what was necessary.

It is very difficult to explain, but as I speak to my friends who have gone through similar experiences, they all agree that they, too, have had similar feelings that defined them in their lives and businesses. When you run out of ways to go, you only take the one road that is ahead of you. You take it and believe in yourself. What you do at that point defines you. It might be taken egoistically, whether you are a strong person or a weak person, but to me it is much simpler than that. Despite what your ego tells you about how you define yourself, think about where you are in life and where you want to be. To me, there is nothing else to it. It is completely emotionless. The only person who cares about your ego is you. Once you let go of self-proclaiming notions, you can take a look at the two options that you are presented with: continue or not. That defines your future.

Not Such A Failure After All

As I am thinking about my bad day here in Barcelona and another upcoming bankruptcy, my third, I think about all of these things. My emotions are screaming at me, saying everything is wrong, but I just let them carry on. I have been here before. I know what I am afraid of, and I know how to fight it. I do not focus on how little time I have. I am focusing on how much time I still have. I am grateful for all of the great experiences my decisions have given me. I have done so much that I have wanted to do that I cannot feel anything but grateful.

Lastly and most importantly, I have my most important assets and my guardians—*patience*, *direction* and *belief*—on my side. As long as I have them, all is good.

Chapter 7
The Yin and Yang of Donald Trump: Finding Your Power in a Tsunami of Hatred

by Karen Higginbottom

Sometimes change bashes you over the head. In my world, there are two types of change. The first is one that we ourselves have either initiated or desired. The second type of change is one that is thrust upon us, undesired, unwelcome, and definitely not initiated by us.

The first type of change can cause many challenges: for example, letting go of old friends who hold us back, or maintaining healthy relationships with family members who don't support the changes that we are trying to make. However, in this chapter, I'm going to focus on the second type of change. The type of change that is brutally thrust upon us, seemingly coming out of nowhere, completely blindsiding us and bringing with it great pain.

This is where I currently am, in a situation that I did not think I'd be in, nor do I want to be in.

What I am about to say next may elicit a reaction from you, most likely judgement. If it does, then I strongly suggest that you keep reading this, for when we are triggered by something, it is merely an indication that there is something unhealed within us, or something that we need to hear. If you observe whatever thoughts or emotions come up and allow them to be, then it can result in great personal insight and deep healing.

So, the situation that I find myself unhappily in is the result of the 2016 general election in the United States of America. If this had been any typical election in the U.S., then personally, having more liberal and Democratic leanings, I wouldn't be thrilled by a Republican getting in to office, but nothing could have prepared me for what was to come. As I write this, we are just seven days into the Trump presidency. If you're already having a reaction to my last couple of sentences, then you are either empathizing with me as you experience a sense of like-minded truth and maybe even some small feelings of relief that you're not alone, or you are already judging me. Maybe you think this event is small and insignificant. You might even be a little angry with what you've just read. In either case, I urge you to read on, being fully aware of your feelings, your thoughts and judgements, as you continue. You may even want to get a piece of paper and a pen and jot down your thoughts and feelings for later self-reflection. If you do this, also jot down where in this chapter those feelings or thoughts arose. When you look back it may help you to gain further insight when you see what it was that triggered those thoughts and feelings within you.

I am a proud member of the Lesbian, Gay, Bisexual, Transgender (LGBT) family. I grew up in the UK, and when I came out, my parents told me that I was no longer welcome at their house and that they would be changing all the locks. I was completely disowned by my parents. While my brother did not initially disown me, he chose to believe the lies that my parents were telling him, so much so that our relationship broke down completely. I also lost aunts and uncles (all of them) and most of my cousins. Why? Simply for having met my soulmate and having fallen in love? I didn't understand this at the time, which is now over ten years ago, and I still don't understand it. How can someone be filled with so much anger—so much hatred—that they disown their own child, their own family member, a part of themselves? I won't lie. This time in my life was really difficult. I had to go through the grieving process, but only worse: they were still alive and actively choosing to shut me out. My sister and brother-in-law stood by me, and still do, for which I am fervently grateful. It took years of crying and processing and grieving to get to a point where it just was, a place where I no longer hated them for disowning me, where I no longer lived in hope that things would improve and that we would reconcile. I finally got to a place of acceptance.

Today, despite no change in those relationships and still being estranged from my parents, I can honestly say that I am even in a place of love for them. This may sound odd, but I realize that I would not be the person I am today had it not been for them. Sometimes a strong negative in our lives can become a strong positive. That's what these were for me. The people that I used to call mum and dad are now just faded memories and are just strangers suffering, empty and emotionless, lonely and lost in the infinity of their minds that are stuck in right and wrong. Be it self-induced or not, how could I not have compassion for them and their suffering? Nobody would consciously choose a life of misery, isolation, criticism, and judgement.

When I moved to the U.S., I did so to be with my now wife. At the time, this was a challenge within itself. If you are not a U.S. citizen, you can't just go and live in the U.S. because you want to. I was fortunate to be consulting for a company that needed somebody with exactly the background that I had, with an understanding of the European healthcare system, to move to the U.S. and service our U.S. based global clients. Upon moving to the U.S., I instantly gained a new family, one that would eventually become my in-laws. They accepted me and I felt their love. I felt part of a family again. I finally felt as though I belonged, and I liked that feeling.

I moved to the U.S. when George W. Bush was president, and, as a same-sex couple, we had no legal rights. Zero. After two to three years together, we wanted to get married, but we were advised against it, as this could be interpreted as showing intent to stay in the U.S. While there were a few states where we could get married, there would have been no federal recognition of our marriage and therefore no immigration. I remember feeling the injustice, the pain and sadness that I couldn't just marry the person that I loved and live in the country that had essentially adopted me. We also faced various legal issues that we had to address. Since there was no legal recognition of our relationship, my girlfriend could easily have been denied access to me should I have been injured in an accident and lying in a coma in hospital. Who did have the legal right of access to me should I be in such a situation? You've guessed correctly: legally my next-of-kin were my parents, the people who had disowned me. So, there were certain things at this time that we had to take care of in an attempt to provide each other and our relationship some sort of basic protections.

In 2009, I saw President Obama take power, and over time our rights as a couple increased. First, in 2013, anyone married in any U.S. state would have their marriage (including same-sex marriages) recognized by the Federal Government. About a year later, same-sex marriage—or simply marriage, as we call it—became law in every state. On both occasions, we cried tears of joy, and we felt true happiness and peace in our hearts. Finally, in 2014, the U.S. had caught up with most of the western world. Needless to say, we became married in 2013. We placed our wedding notice in the local newspapers for each of our families, and in 2013 we were the first same-sex couple in each paper to have its wedding announced. Then, in 2014, following the decision by the Supreme Court that ruled in favor of full same-sex marriage rights, one of our wedding pictures was front page in the local U.S. paper along with an interview where a local journalist interviewed my wife on her thoughts and what the ruling meant. It was a time of joy, acceptance, and of equality. At least in the eyes of the law.

As I sit here writing this now, that hope, joy, and peace has faded. We now have a president who has appointed a white supremacist to a very senior position of power, and we have rabidly anti-LGBT individuals that have been chosen as cabinet picks, people who either have already been or are waiting to be appointed to high-level government positions. Under the guise of religious freedom, anti-LGBT laws appear to have been drafted and are just moments away from being passed by this new majority Republican government.

If you voted for our current President and cannot understand what the problem is, then maybe you can help me. I frequently hear the standard rhetoric from people that voted for Trump as they say they are not racist and they are not homophobic; they just wanted change. But I see no proof of this. We, the minority groups—women, LGBT, people of color*, the black community, Muslims and immigrants—need to see congruency from people. We want to believe friends and family members when they tell us that they are not racist or homophobic. But we do not see these same people taking actions to denounce this. Surely, if what we are being told is true, we would be seeing social media posts saying things like, "I voted for Trump but I do not support the appointment of a white supremacist to the president's inner circle." We believe in a president for everyone, not just a president for the white, straight, Christian, wealthy male. We certainly don't want a president that is celebrated by the leaders of the KKK who post "Hail Prez Trump!" on social media. Even more shocking, the KKK announced they "enthusiastically endorse the aggressive anti-Black racist," the president's pick for Attorney General.

If, by your own admission, you are...

Racist (a person who shows or feels discrimination or prejudice against people of other races, or who believes that a particular race is superior to another);

Homophobic (having or showing a dislike of, or prejudice against, homosexual people);

Transphobic (a range of antagonistic attitudes and feelings against transgender or transsexual people); sexist (relating to or characterized by prejudice, stereotyping, or discrimination, typically against women, on the basis of gender);

Islamophobic (fear, prejudice, hatred, or dislike directed against Islam or Muslims, or towards Islamic politics or culture); **a misogynist** (a person who dislikes, despises, or is strongly prejudiced against women; or **xenophobic** (having or showing a dislike of, or prejudice against, people from other countries)…

…then that is a different matter and should be one for self-exploration as to where those beliefs came from and why you choose to keep them. I almost guarantee that they are not your own beliefs but the beliefs of others or of the media. You see, they need people like you to buy into their belief system to further promote their own self-interests. Even if you personally suffered a crime at the hands of a person from one of these minority groups, it is unlikely that you would generalize that crime into hating a whole group of people. It is, however, likely possible that you have one of the following three things going on.

1. You cannot accept that which is in yourself; e.g. the people that are the most homophobic and vocal about it often turn out to be the ones questioning their own sexual orientations, or are having thoughts of a same-sex sexual nature that they cannot reconcile because they have bought into the propaganda of conservative Christianity, which over time they have accepted as their own beliefs. But that is just a religious belief system, based on a book which has been manipulated throughout the ages to control the population at large at any given time and to promote the self-serving interests of various groups and churches that have been in power. Think about it from a basic level of, God is loving. If you fall into this category of not being able to accept that which is within you, and you had absolute knowing and a palpable, undeniable connection with God, who told you to be happy, to love and accept yourself, and to be kind to yourself, how would your life change? What would you do differently? How would your self-talk change if you accepted and loved all of yourself?

2. For some reason (be it abuse, self-doubt, fear, neglect, negative thinking, wanting to belong, or to be part of something bigger), over the course of your life so far you have felt small, have developed a low self-esteem, and you have felt less than that which you truly are. Nobody wants to feel that way, and in an ideal world nobody should. It's not nice to feel less than others, and if you find yourself falling into this category and you address this, it can bring up deep parts of the emotionally unhealed psyche. This can be very painful to feel and to admit, let alone to know what to do with these feelings or how to move through them and heal them. It's much easier to point at a group or groups of people and make them wrong and to make all of your problems or all of the country's problems exist because of them rather than to admit your own feelings of lack and insecurity.

3. Unhealed anger. A lot of people have unhealed anger similar in nature to the second point above. It's much easier to project that anger onto others, be it partners, spouses, work colleagues, or general groups of minorities, than it is to face healing the anger that keeps bubbling to the surface. One could make the argument that this last point is simply a deeper layer of the second point above. Often, when we do self-introspection, we find that issues of anger are merely trying to protect us from feeling the depths of our pain and sadness.

Regardless of your political beliefs, or even in which country you reside, if you can honestly say that you are not racist, homophobic, sexist, a misogynist, Islamophobic, or xenophobic, then, whether you actually realize it yet or not, you are in fact about to face a dilemma. If you live in a country where any of these beliefs are accepted in any way, shape, or form, then the dilemma is, do you turn a blind eye and do nothing? After all, it's not your problem; you are not a part of these minority groups. Or do you examine yourself and look within and do what you, deep down in your being, know is right? If you know the truth of what you must do, then without exception stand up. Stand up for what is right—not against racism, homophobia, sexism, Islamophobia, misogyny, or xenophobia—but stand up FOR 100% equality for ALL people.

If you've never stood up before, then just reading this may bring up some fear in you. If that's the case, then start small. But start. Simply clicking 'like' on a social media post that someone has posted pointing out the injustice of a particular legislation or an antiquated cultural belief system can begin to make a big difference. Or reach out to a friend or family member who may be marginalized and let them know that you are thinking of them, even if you admit that you don't yet fully understand. Let them know that you care enough about them to want to understand. This lets that person know that they are not alone, and it's the beginning of you allowing yourself to open up to the possibility of seeing the world through the eyes of another. Begin to read the articles that are being presented from the perspective of the other person and try to understand why people may be feeling unsafe, afraid, or worried. Seek to understand and experience why they are hurting.

Taking my own advice, I have also used this very same approach in the current situation that has seemingly caused so much turmoil. I have looked at why this might have happened, and I must admit that there was a small part of me that had known this was possible. People wanted change. Hillary Clinton did not bring any promise of that. She was just a different face that represented more of the same old political system. Also, Hillary Clinton focused a lot of her campaign on STOPPING Trump. So the focus from the Trump campaign was on Trump, while the focus from the Clinton campaign was also on Trump.

I want to acknowledge that, as I look from a different perspective, I can already see that some good has occurred from the Trump presidency. It is my belief (from what I understand) the rejecting of the Trans-Pacific Partnership (TPP) trade agreement is a beneficial thing. (If you're interested and haven't heard of it, or don't know what the TPP trade agreement was/is about, then google it and read more.) I'm also aware that there is a much stronger sense of unity among many people as well. This feeling of standing together, and standing up for one another is much stronger than I have ever seen. Although the unity is mainly from people opposing Trump's ideas, we are also starting to see social media posts from people who voted for Trump and are now disillusioned and upset. Big picture view: The actions of President Trump are actually uniting many people on both sides.

I also acknowledge that, from a deeper perspective, all of this needed to come out and come to the surface. The racism and homophobia was always there, present in a lot of people. It was just buried below the surface. The Trump victory allowed all of this to come out into the open. People now feel justified, that it's their right to express all of this anger and hatred with all of the bigotry spewing out of them onto whatever minority group is currently within sight. What if this is actually a good thing?

When infection is inside the body, the illusion of external appearance is that things are okay, maybe even good. A flow of putrid puss gushing out of a wound gives the appearance that things are now much worse. We all understand that, for the wound and the body to heal, all of that infection has to come out. Just like an addict who is hiding his addiction can't be helped, the first step toward healing anything is to bring it to light. All of this putrid infection of anger, hatred, racism, homophobia, and separation needed to come out. Symbolically, the wound is America, which is oozing puss before the country can heal. Until the wound heals, the body cannot. I believe that the body, represented by our world and collective human consciousness is ready to heal.

Looking back at my own situation, I can see now that I had also hidden and suppressed things from myself. I had seen things through my own rose-tinted glasses. The new family that I so craved and longed for, that

I had gained, my now in-laws, had truly accepted me as much as they were capable of. They loved me as much as they could. But if I'm fully honest, I've minimized quite a few of our interactions over the years, suppressing my own sadness and my own anger at some of the things that were either said or not said. I was told by one family member, on quite a few occasions, that she didn't think my wife and I had the right to be married and how it was against God. I think back to how I sat there listening to this, wondering if there was anything that I could say that would have the ability to open her mind, even just a fraction. Very gently, I did try a few different perspectives, but I could see that in the moment her need to feel better than at least a couple of other people was strong. This led her to letting me know, very bluntly at times, that the marriage of my wife and me (the first for both of us) wasn't real, and in her opinion it was much less significant than her two previous God-endorsed heterosexual marriages. Seeing and recognizing her pain, I refrained from getting angry or quoting the Bible back at her to destroy her arguments. I just sat there, on various occasions listening, still loving her.

I also had to come to terms with, admitting to myself, how difficult it was when we got engaged. We couldn't just be in the joy of our engagement. We had to strategize about how we were going to announce our engagement to my new family in order to minimize experiencing the sadness and pain that, real or perceived, we would feel coming from fake and forced congratulations or—even worse—the silence of disapproval. We waited a few weeks before telling anyone so that we could combine the announcement of our engagement with a party that we were throwing for my sister and her husband, who I knew would be happy that the focus of the party was no longer solely on them. I remember seeing who at the party just walked away after our announcement while others were walking towards us to congratulate us. I remember the people there that night who couldn't even utter the words "I'm happy for you both."

The Yin and Yang of Donald Trump: Finding Your Power in a Tsunami of Hatred

I remember planning a wedding without any guests because we couldn't face the pain of seeing people in our family trying to come up with legitimate sounding excuses as to why they couldn't make it. We knew that some of them just didn't believe we should be able to get married. I remember the kind gift of money towards our wedding from my mother-in-law and experiencing the feelings of joy and appreciation, but then also the feelings of sadness and confusion at finding out that all of my other siblings had also been given money. This seemed odd; why was this? Was it a common family tradition that when the parents paid for, or gave a financial gift towards the wedding of one of their children that all the other children also received money? Apparently not, just for ours.

And then, just like the Symbol of the Tao (also known as the Tai Chi or Yin Yang symbol) which represents the balance between two opposites and visually expresses the concept of darkness within the light, and the presence of light in the darkness, each opposite giving rise to the other, inextricably linked in the ebb and flow of life like the changing of the seasons, my new family threw us a celebratory wedding dinner party.

Thanksgiving, 2013, was just over a month after we were married. The whole family was together and they expressed their love and acknowledgement of us, our union and our love. This gesture was truly appreciated and we felt their love for us. Along with corsage flowers there were even gifts for us: scarves, games, a picture frame, and a beautiful metallic piece of art made by a local artist. Of all the items from that evening, my favorite was actually one of the decorations. For our party it adorned the wooden mantle at my sister-in-law's home where we had gathered. Our niece had made a banner of bunting that had our names and wedding date on it. To this day, it still hangs in our hallway on what we call our wedding wall, where pictures and memories of our wedding hang. When we announced our engagement, unbeknownst to me, my godmother began working on an exquisite hand embroidered picture.

After we were married she had it framed and sent to us as a permanent reminder of our wedding. This also hangs on the same wall.

As I write about the hand embroidered gift from my godmother, I realize that in the beginning of this chapter, as I talked about coming out, I focused on what I had lost and I failed to acknowledge the positive, the people that had stood by me, that had been supportive and had reached out to me. My godparents were in this category: fun, kind, and utterly decent people that enjoyed life. Also in this category were numerous friends, many that I didn't get to see as often as I would like, but that were unfaltering in their friendship and support, as were a few of my cousins. A couple of weeks following our wedding, my wife and I were in London celebrating our marriage. The outpouring of love was palpable as about 40 of our closest friends and family celebrated with us.

It's relatively easy to see what is wrong, what is unjust, and how people have let us down. What's more difficult to realize and certainly to acknowledge is what is right. Where have people been there for us that we've maybe taken for granted? How often do we acknowledge to ourselves the real value of the friendship or family relationships and express just how much they really mean to us?

Other aspects for consideration: Have we recognized our own role in this situation? How would a neutral observer view this dynamic of interaction?

I can clearly see that my new family is made of people who really do care and love us, but I now also see that there has long been a disconnection. We are not fully accepted or celebrated as a married couple, but then again our views on life and how we see the world are also very different. It's much easier to fully accept someone who thinks and believes the same way we do. So, when we feel unaccepted, perhaps we haven't fully accepted all of them either. I saw how I had judged their judgements as being uninformed or resulting from misinformation. I had judged that their views of the world were somehow narrower than mine rather than just different. All of this is what I had previously simply refused to see, or I had seen it momentarily and then had chosen to forget about it. I just suppressed and minimized it. I had put all these events out of mind because they were too painful. I hadn't allowed myself to fully feel the pain, the anger and the sadness of these situations. I had denied my own reality, choosing to believe it was something other than what it really was.

If I bring all of this back to my current situation and my current reality, then I can choose to see that Trump's and the nation's anger is just a big gigantic mirror for me—and others if they choose—to take a long look at the anger within myself (ourselves) and to learn to fully accept that darkness, the Yin. Light, the Yang, cannot exist without its equal and opposite partner of duality, which is the darkness, to provide the contrast. I had understood this world of duality for a long time, but now I appreciate that the anger, the darkness, the Yin, in and of itself, is also perfect in its own existence.

Anger, when used correctly, can be a very powerful and effective tool, not only to help bring about the change that we desire, but also to lead us to a place of really loving ourselves. What I could very clearly now see was that previously—in any moment when anger arose within me—in that moment, it was actually a healthy anger, but in the very process of denying and quickly suppressing it, it became toxic, unhealed, and a truth that I was refusing to accept.

I now perceive that healthy in-the-moment anger is a way Self tries to communicate with me, as if to say this is not okay; you deserve more. You deserve love, acceptance, and to be truly cherished and celebrated for who you are.

We all deserve this. Each of us has just taken a different journey to discover our own truths and to come to our own realizations and beliefs, where we understand that we are truly deserving of it.

Now my final thoughts regarding change are, not that there are two types of change, but there are in fact three.

1. There is the type of change that we ourselves have either initiated or desired.

2. There is the type of change that is thrust upon us, undesired, unwelcomed and definitely not initiated by us. However, for our own health and best long-term outcome, it is one in which we must fully accept in its entirety exactly as it is: e.g. the sudden, unexpected death of a loved one. This type of change can take some getting used to. Sadly, and maybe heartbrokenly, we experience the death of a loved one or the irreparable breakup of a relationship.

3. Finally, there is the type of change that is thrust upon us, undesired, unwelcome, and definitely not initiated by us. But this type of change requires people to listen to, or find, their own truths and to stand up for their beliefs. This type of change should be both accepted and not accepted at the same time. (I accept that Donald Trump is currently the president of the United States of America, but I do NOT accept bullying and the singling out of minority groups. I do not accept injustice and discrimination.) In this case, only when people stand up and reject the status quo does real change occur.

When you are called by your own truth to stand against or to resist something, then I actually recommend that you don't. Yes, you read that correctly. After just telling you that this type of change needs people to stand up, I have just contradicted myself by saying do NOT stand up AGAINST that which you do not want. This is because it is so much more powerful and impactful to stand FOR what you DO want. This may seem like a subtle or irrelevant distinction, but it is not. It's a powerful one. Do not stand up against racism and homophobia, but stand up and speak out for equality, for inclusion, and for peace and justice.

I would like you to ponder, for yourself, the following questions:

- What in your life is worth fighting for?
- What in your life is worth dying for?
- What in your life is worth living for?

To me, there is only one answer: Love. And in the eyes of love, everyone is equal.

Please note that the term people of color (POC) is an acceptable term embraced and used by this broader community within the U.S. In many countries outside of the US this phrase would be considered derogatory and racist. It is obviously used here as intended in the former, as a descriptive catch-all term referring to anyone that looks anything other than white. While I could have just used the widely accepted ethnic term Caucasian instead of white, even that terminology has its origins rooted within racism.

Chapter 8
In the Now Is Love: Reconnecting in Love
By Zbigniew Tappert

Sometimes I guess we require the darkness before we can appreciate the light. I might have often confused the darkness by calling it my light, but, then, over and over again, I had to realize that different names do not change things. Writing this came from a place of deep darkness which I felt right before I started. However, what I've discovered has made me feel extremely satisfied with the now and with me and with wanting to never leave this state again. It has made me feel like the better person that I was, but, most of all, I learned who I am by connecting with it. It– this thing I learned—made me feel rich on my life's journey and this is what I would like to share with you, since I believe this intelligence is a part of who we all are.

This is what turned out to be my very own *Journey of Riches*.

My life from the outside has always looked good. I was successful. I had a career. I was travelling and living around the world, always surrounded with fantastic people and blessed with loving family and friends. But, at the same time, I started feeling disconnected on the inside.

There were many aspects leading to this, I guess. I'd learned a lot when travelling and living around the world, by meeting people, by understanding their different ways of life, by realizing what's important to them, by looking into different belief systems than my own and seeing what was right and wrong to different people. I guess it all became too much for me to comprehend, especially combined with the online world which constantly told me what's good for everyone. I just didn't know anymore how to identify what was good for me or what is the right thing to do and how to prevent myself from doing what is wrong. And the more I attempted to identify and live it, the deeper I failed.

I felt like I couldn't stop becoming another me. I felt as if the real me had died somewhere along the way and I didn't understand where or when or why. I didn't know how to get it back. Life went on and I had to live with this new me and try to accept him and adapt to new situations, but, at the same time, I missed who I used to be, who I felt I really was. I had become quite vulnerable to others as well as to myself and had developed this inner hatred towards myself.

I'd become very hard on myself. As if I was testing the new me I'd become, I was never satisfied, always looking for more and expecting more than I could ever prove myself to be able to give. This inner hatred and blame were leading to a constantly growing dissatisfaction with myself. I didn't like, let alone love, anything about myself. I learned that, in turn, this resulted in my poor relations with everything and everyone else. I desperately needed to live my own life. I needed to reconnect. But how? With whom? Who am I? Who are we all anyway?

The distance was getting longer and longer. The distance between the me I hated—by whom I identified myself—and the me I'd love to be again but had totally forgotten about. Who is he? Where is he? I felt disconnected from me and thus from life.

I really began to worry, since I had no more dreams like I used to have. Dreams used to be my most powerful tool for creating my life. But when I felt disconnected, I could not think of anything that felt like a genuine dream to me. Even though I had plans and made decisions about what I wanted to achieve, these didn't feel like they were my own. Before, dreams just came my way naturally and in the same way they would always come true. But when I felt disconnected, it felt as if I were supposed to do something that was not my own. I didn't like those new dreams. They didn't feel like mine, and this led to discrepancies between what I wanted and what I am, thus never leading to fulfilment, as dreams do not come true when our inner defense mechanisms are strong enough to prevent them from actualization. So, I failed most of the time, gave up or procrastinated, because it wasn't me; it was this new person I hated, this other person who made the decisions for me. It was easier for me to work for others.

So, instead of dreaming for myself and living my own dream, I would work for money while making other people's dreams and visions come true. And, yes, I enjoyed the work, and I was really good at it whenever I was left to work very creatively and independently, from a place of respect and understanding of the situations and people I dealt with, as we came up with great solutions for our businesses. People were often very supportive and we developed mutual attitudes of respect, which was good for all of us. I loved to coach the people I managed, too.

But then I had to deal with this other boss who didn't know any better than to just tell me what to do and wouldn't be bothered anymore. It is when you're disconnected from your true self that others can take advantage of you. I realized that I was not a machine or a servant. And I became fully aware that I was just working on someone else's dream instead of being a part of it or owning it. More and more I felt like my freedom became my greatest value to embrace. And I quit my job.

Did that help me in any way? Embracing the freedom felt good—it opened some doors—but then I still felt disconnected from who I felt I really was. I think that, after quitting my job and throwing myself into the deep waters of the unknown, I first found myself in a situation in which I could breathe again. But after a while, I would tell myself what to do all the time, just like I knew it from my work. The pressure I felt was getting stronger and stronger and I was being harder and harder on myself. I felt like I wasn't moving anywhere. I kind of knew what to do to make it right, but I failed most of the time.

Now, after reflection, I see that I was trying to be my own boss and tell myself what to do, the same kind of situation I'd tried to avoid at work. I quit my job, but how can I quit my own life? And I've been thinking about it. I hated my own bossy self. Zee, I quit! It doesn't work like that. And I would hate myself even more, be harder on myself and think of myself as a person I should avoid but couldn't. One way of dealing with it would be to end it all and I had to remind myself why I shouldn't. There was but little of me in the reasons I could come up with. Nevertheless, since I decided to live, there was no point of feeling like a dead man walking. So I kept searching.

I would listen to many people and read many books saying how important it was to love yourself and to be grateful for everything. It felt better for a while but, then again, I would stumble and fall into my own dark hole. I never got the point of loving myself. This idea has been continuously rejected by my inner mission control. It sounded selfish and when I looked at myself, when I observed my life, I asked for a reason why I should do it when I'm not perfect, when I was doing all of these strange and silly things, or when I look the way I do. It just didn't click with me. But this was always my question: why can't I be somebody I can love? I tried to become that person but never could.

At some point I began to ask myself, why does everybody love the little babies, especially right after they are born? I haven't seen anybody whose heart would not genuinely warm up when they saw babies during the first days of their lives. When I was a kid, I often wanted to be older, to have what I have now, to be who I am now. And now I'm wondering why people love little babies and I can't love myself. Why don't we love ourselves like we love little children? This question alone led me onto a journey of self-discovery.

Searching for the real me somewhere in my life, searching for the stage when my dreams were still an inseparable part my life's purpose, I could not help but move deeper and deeper through many thick layers of what I felt had formed some sort of cocoon around me. I became more aware of how those layers had been defining who I am for a long time. It's as if a Gucci bag could define who people are, a lame concept of the 20th century.

By going deeper and farther back into my own life, I found that the further I go, the more sense it makes, the stronger it gets—this discovery I was heading towards—until I discover the greatest revelation for me. It literally struck me when I saw it, when I understood clearly how huge it was and how powerful, and also what an idiot I'd been since it had been available to me all the time. This is also when it dawned on me: the magnitude of the distance between who I identified myself with through the wonderful-looking cocoon I found myself inside of and the true power source of Life I suddenly saw.

I felt as stupid as a battery-powered rabbit that thinks he doesn't work or switch off, but all it takes is the on/off switch on his bum, right underneath his cute little tail, and off he twerks.

What I'm talking about, what I saw, was when this glimpse of a moment that I understood happened, just when my body was in its slimmest condition—right before I started putting on weight—a process that never stopped. This was the moment when life was given to me. I understand that something happened beyond any form of physical or biological explanation. And I believe it was a moment which cannot be measured in time. It just happened. At this moment, I was filled with life which came from a place of love where nothing is just possible but, instead, everything simply is.

When I imagine it, the extent of its power seems endless to me. The love coming from it is so pure and so unconditional that there is also something I cannot describe when I look at it. It's like this space of opportunities, of everything possible, of all there is, even though I think "all" is a limited term and what I saw should not be limited in any way. It's as if there must be many more colors to what we know, as if our experiences here were only a tiny little bean in an endless garden of constantly available situations where it all happens at the same time. Right now I really feel like a twerking rabbit.

Whenever I imagine this very moment I was given life, I can see the wholeness of life through the eyes of the baby who experiences it at this moment, when everything is new, when everything is now. And then it strikes me again: I am this baby after all. I have always been. It is like time travel really.

There I am with tiny little muscles, exposed private parts, and promising looks, filled with the most exquisite gift ever available to human kind. I'm taking my first breath and screaming my lungs out loud as if there were no neighbors. And, baby, just check out the body! I mean, just look at me! Mother Nature worked her back parts off for me to be born with trillions of cells combined into a fully functional, custom-designed organism. No need for copyrights; there is no one else like me or you! Nowadays, inventors work on robots and artificial intelligence. And we automatically move most of our body parts already, whereas the intelligence proves its presence with time, I guess, but we are more sophisticated and working better than anything that can be designed and engineered these days. If that doesn't make us feel good about where we came from and who we have materialized to be, what else would? In that sense, I am perfect. And so is everybody else.

Now, in the book The Little Prince by Antoine de Saint-Exupéry, Little Prince once said, "But you must not forget it. You become responsible, forever, for what you have tamed. You are responsible for your rose." And I needed reminding of the truth. I remembered again when I saw myself on this very first moment of my life. I look myself in the eyes, and the child looks back. And I see myself in him. And in my eyes, in this very moment when life is being given to me, I see the ultimate experience of being, the most pleasant love I've ever felt, the gratefulness expressed with joy, the perfect awareness of now as well as the gifts I was equipped with, like hardware tools you get for your birthday. I feel the power of it all emanating through me, and it is such a blessing to be there and experience this miracle we call life.

And, at the same time, I realize that I am solely responsible for this child. At this moment, the child looks at me. The eyes open a bit wider. The grin on his face slowly dissolves, gradually allowing for a slight but significant jaw drop. There comes the moment when the world stops turning. He gently lifts his head towards me, and after a few seconds of looking into my right, then left, then right eye again, he whispers in my face, "What da fuk?"

This is the most important confrontation, the moment for me to understand if what I've been doing to myself, to this child, has been good or not. Knowing that I am a product of love, coming where I come from, having what was given to me, which is endless and whole—when I face myself, I feel a lot of love and a lot of responsibility for doing the right thing. Maybe this is the responsibility parents feel towards their children. I feel that towards myself when I come from the place where I feel myself now. This gives me the best perspective to view what I've been doing or who I was becoming through my experiences or allowances thereof. That's because I am either good to myself, meaning the baby child, or not. It's that simple to me.

This is what I'm calling stripping off my cocoon, which I've noticed on my way to discovering the child. The cocoon reveals itself. Sometimes I don't understand my own reactions, my handling of things. Lessons I've learned, one by one, have created tools for me to live past those events. There are so many things making my cocoon colorful and thick. Oftentimes I feel constrained by it, though. I cannot move outside of it;

instead, I use it as my personal shield against what's outside. By being inside of it, I identify myself with it, which then creates the vicious cycle. To get out of it, I must either strip myself completely of it or directly connect with the source of me as the child in this very first moment life is given to me and be the child. Or allow the child to be through me.

Stripping off without yet connecting to the source can be revealing, healing, interesting, and fun all at the same time. Let's analyze and strip off a few of those layers as an exercise in revelation.

One layer I've always worn is, I am fat!

"What da fuk!" I hear the child exclaim already. But then if I go right before this embarrassing moment, I see the child as pure love and trusting me with his life. Then I have to explain to him that I am going to make him fat and hate him for it! So, I go "Listen, baby Zee. You are all there is and pure love, and what I am going to do with you is to hate you for something I'll do to you. How do you feel about that?"

I can see the baby's head lifting towards me already, but before I hear the famous words, I continue with my rumination. Let's see where this belief was born. One day, I explain to him, you will be six years old. And after not seeing your friends for a long while, you'll decide to go and play with them again. You will walk downstairs, two floors down from your parents' apartment, open the front door and you see them: your friends! Happy day! We will play again! You walk towards them, and, by maybe the ninth or tenth step you take, they see you, look at you, and one of them yells, "You are fat!" And they laugh.

My life, beginning from that 11th step onwards, would never be the same. I guess, right then and there, I registered that being fat is considered something bad, something others can judge you and belittle you for, something that should make you feel bad about yourself. It took me another 15 or 16 steps before I reached them, and by then I had already recorded in my head that I was fat and that this should make me feel bad about myself.

I am quite sure that my friends would not remember that moment. They probably forgot it as soon as they'd said it. We continued playing. I remember that we were playing with grey sand. I think it was the beginning of spring: no green, still a bit cold, and we were wearing thick grey jackets. There were three of us. I remember it all vividly. And I see and experience it over and over again every time I look in the mirror. Regardless if I am fat or not, I see it; it's programmed in my mind like an automatic functioning switch. Every single day, every single time I look in the mirror, there is nothing else I see. I've accepted it. This is who I am.

The baby carefully lifts his head towards me, tilting it slightly. "Why?" "Who are you?" I imagine him questioning.

When I face the precious child, I realize who I am. When I tell the story, I see the responsibility of my own decisions about the child. I've been irresponsible enough to treat this amazing product of life and love with such hatred. Would you hate a little baby the moment it is born? Well, it seems I did!

And then the baby helps me. In a way, I feel an invitation to connect again to all there is, to all the good that the baby is. This is me after all. And I can reconnect to it and feel good about it all again. Had I been able to do this when I took my 11th step, then maybe I wouldn't have had to deal with the problem of hating myself all my life just for how I looked. Maybe I would not have gotten fat again every time I lost weight, because this fat child would not be who I was identifying myself with. Maybe. But I could not, and I did hate my fat self.

I was just a child and couldn't really handle the ridicule all that well, and I allowed it to take over my life. This is why sharing awareness about bullying and preventing it are so important to me. For me, it's good to make this distinction even after 32 years. And I guess I'm almost at my fattest stage of life now, but looking at it from a perspective of the child that is connected in love with me again after I told him the truth about it has releases me from this identity. So long, trauma. One cocoon layer is gone.

What else bothers me? My money situation. The definition of people based on their status in life is completely irrelevant to reality. I know so many rich people and they are awesome, or not, but money does not define that. However, it has always defined me. To me. And in turn it defines my money situation. I can't have it all. Imagine telling your baby child at the first moment he's born, coming from a place of never ending abundance, that he cannot have it all.

"What da Fuk?"

So, when does it start? I can see my parents struggling and still giving me all they could. And this is it. I just realized, this is it. I am doing exactly the same thing. I now know I can have what I want, but I need to struggle, too. Mies van der Rohe's "less is more" perfectly describes this ridiculous program in my head and its huge effect on my life.

I learned jealousy as a kid. I experienced this emotion regularly as I was growing up with the belief that others had more than me. Pewex was one of the stores in my home town. I think my nose was smudging horizontal lines over its windows twice a day. It was the little America. You had to have dollars to shop in this store. I remember Matchbox cars in 1:64 scale, police cars, fire trucks, all of those little things I knew I couldn't have. There was Lego as well. I can compare looking at Lego Technics back then as a child to watching naked bodies now as an adult. It felt good. There was chocolate, too. I looked at people who were buying from there, and I thought to myself, Why them? Why not me? And I accepted it, and myself, in this scenario.

I guess it wouldn't be so harmful if I hadn't developed the state of jealousy combined with an excuse for me to say, "These people are bad and I am good." It was an equivalent for me to say, "These people are rich and I am poor. They have; I don't." And then I would hear many people saying, "Those who have money are not good people. They are cheaters. Money is evil. It doesn't make you happy."

And I wanted to be good. I was taught not to cheat, to act with love, and I desperately wanted to be happy. So, all of a sudden, money became something out of reach for me, something I learned not to even want, something I would protect myself from.

And is money really bad? Does it make you a bad person? Well, I've seen that happen, but I've also met the most beautiful rich people who were just like all of the other good people, except that they had the ability to do more good in the material world we live in, for themselves as well as for others.

So, I go to the baby and I say, "For as long as I remember, and I guess it's 35 years now, I've kept you poor to protect you." The baby takes a deep breath, exhales, looks up at the ceiling, lifts his little hand up high, then drops it while the palm slaps his forehead.

I have never been poor. In fact, there were times when I had more money than I was spending, and I was spending a lot. Maybe I was spending so much because I wanted to get rid of it all, as I didn't want to be considered a bad person. But, in general, having money is similar to being fat. Even when I look at my pictures from a few years back when I look pretty much slim, I still felt fat. And when I look back at the times when I had money, I still felt poor.

It's good to acknowledge where limiting beliefs come from, since this programming will remind me of its existence in my brain a few more times before I rid myself of it. But re-connecting to the child, coming from a place of full abundance where all opportunities are already happening, and being accepted by the child again—since all we need in order to be accepted is just to make a wish for it to be so—there is no resentment, just pure and unconditional love to me, from me, from life. This experience truly heals me and destroys the cocoon's layer that has been my money pattern, all as if it had never existed.

Now, when I think of it, I see money as a game we can play for fun and for those beautiful things we can make with it. I see it as an opportunity rather than a hindrance. I feel free and full of energy now. There are no grey clouds over my head anymore. Instead there is the beautiful breeze of chances for me to grab onto and play with.

The child opens his eyes while we're spooning in love, looks in front of himself, and shakes his head in disbelief that this is really happening. But, yes, I just came back from this ridiculous trip I've been on. I'm home. Eyes close.

I could go on with these stories. I could unfold each part of the cocoon that still exists, and probably I will, either consciously or as particular situations occur. It does free me; it literally lets me move again in the abundance of the life I was given.

But I can also skip this part altogether and feel good. I can directly reconnect with the child, again reminding myself of the glimpse of a moment when this awesomeness of life got pumped into my body to prove that I'm worth it. I'm worth living and using all of the tools I was given for whatever reason I need or want them. In this moment, I am everything. And I am made of love. And I love that! And I love the fact that this is me! This is who I am.

Every time I remember this, I remember how I felt in the good times— in the times when I dreamt and in those times when the dreams were coming true, in the times when I created. It is interesting for me to observe how design and creativity impact this awareness, and also the other way around, how my awareness and being in the now with love triggers and influences my creativity and design.

And the creations were coming through me as if I were just a messenger and a tool for them to materialize in this world. In the times when I danced and felt this deep connection with music, as if my body were in harmony with the energy. In the times when I played piano without thinking of any notes, but instead allowed for emotions and thoughts to create the music in me first, which my hands then translated onto the keyboard. In the times when I was taking and editing pictures, which captured my emotions and their interpretation of the real world, rather than just what I saw with my eyes. In the times when I loved and the love was vibrating through me to be expressed in passion and the indescribable connection of bodies and souls.

This feeling is my meditation. I meditate through creation. This is my tool. I've got it again, but I must admit that I disconnected from it for a long time because of my inability to keep creating my life from the position of who I was, allowing myself to accept that there is better and I am worse.

What all of this caused is, I decided for myself that I could not dream anymore and I thought that all of my dreams had already come true. I decided for myself that I was not good enough to create, and there are better creators anyway. I decided for myself that I shouldn't dance any longer, since I must look ridiculous. I had a piano but never played. I decided that I needed to learn how to do it properly first, which I never did, since this didn't feel like mine anymore. I decided that my good times in photography were over. I had become accomplished enough to achieve some recognition for my work, but I am not good enough; there are many others doing the same thing and more successfully. I still took photos, but these did not feel the same anymore. I decided for myself that I am not good enough to be loved for who I am. If I cannot love me, how can somebody else love me? I found myself often blaming the other person for things that I interpreted as being done just to cause me more pain, to punish me for not being lovable. (That's a tough one!)

But then there is this creation of life that I feel—this child being born whom I automatically connect to now whenever I think of it. I am that I am. There is nothing I am not. And where it comes from is the abundance of everything, the wealth of love, the richness of...me. And everything I had decided was wrong about me before now dissolves. And I am good again. I live from a state of joy and love. The love must turn towards myself before I can ever love anybody else.

There is this beautiful verse from the Bible,

Matthew 19:14: "Let the little children come to me, and do not hinder them, for the kingdom of heaven belongs to such as these."

And Matthew 18:3: "Truly I tell you, unless you change and become like little children, you will never enter the kingdom of heaven."

I hindered the child that I am. But that child comes from the kingdom of heaven, and this is where he belongs. By allowing him to live, I allow for heaven to have its place right here and now.

This is the most beautiful meditation for me now, which I understand gets stronger with practice. And it is my own responsibility to be myself and to practice the reconnection often enough to never become disconnected again.

So, to wrap it up, I think my Journey of Riches goes backwards first, to discover that this is where I was, and still am, the richest I can ever be. This is the beginning, every day to be grateful for the blessing of the moment life was given to me and my chance to experience whatever one can experience on this planet through the material form of my body, which—regardless of fat or slim, dark or bright, tall or small, even handicapped or not—we are here to experience the truth about ourselves, and we must learn as well as unlearn the lies that hinder us from it.

Then I would look at the child, smile, and say, "There is someone else I'd like you to meet." And I'd point at a person approaching us slowly. The closer he gets, the better the child understands that this is him: this is us. This guy is me on the last day of my life—actually, right at the very moment when life is being taken out of me to bring it back to the kingdom of heaven, if you will. He is the indication that this life experience is over at some point. And he becomes our best friend, the one who not only wishes us all the good there is to experience but also the one who is wise and knows it all already. Every time I look up to him, I can ask him—ask myself really—if this is the right way for me to go, if this experience is bringing me closer to where I am going, if this decision is right or what is the right decision for the goals I've set. He loves me just the way I love the child I am. He is responsible for me. He tamed me and I feel safe. He is my big brother. He is me.

By connecting to both of my selves in the very first moment I was given life and at the very last when the life will continue where it came from, I feel that this not only makes my journey complete, but, by enjoying what abundance I am a part of, it also makes me feel rich, as we all are richer than I had ever felt before understanding this experience we call life.

Chapter 9
Falling Into Change
By Isabella Verzberger

I was 11 years old, long before any endeavors toward my journey to sucess began, and I already faced a gauntlet of horrifying obstacles. This is my story.

I was at a school in Israel where I had a Yemenite teacher who hated me. She would belittle me in front of everyone. When my mother confronted her, the woman was obnoxious and told her to go back to Russia to the KGB and die.

This woman was aware that my mother was born in Moldova, which was a part of the former Soviet Union.

I come from a family of holocaust survivors. The brothers and sisters of both of my grandfathers perished in the holocaust. My grandparents were survivors from Auschwitz and Treblinka. Was this the reason I wasn't good enough?

I always wondered why my teacher hated me. I was very thin but I wasn't bad looking. I loved science. It was my passion, and I wanted to be a veterinarian. But my teacher told me I didn't have much of a chance in life and that I should forget about my dreams of being a vet and especially a scientist. It would be impossible for me. She would say nasty things, like the world would be a better place without me. I was ashamed and hurt, crying in the washroom, but I never cried in front of her.

I was really shy and uncomfortable inside my own skin. I was always afraid of her. Whenever I had migraines, she would audaciously say, "Good. You should drop dead!" When I was in class one day, my migraines were so bad, that I started to have a nose bleed. Luckily, the boys in my class liked me, and they rushed to the principle to call the paramedics. My mother eventually transferred me to another school. I later heard that my former teacher died from brain cancer six months later.

But my problems didn't end there. In my new school, I had a French teacher who was hostile towards me. She accused me of cheating on exams. But as time moved on, I grew in confidence until the day came when I could stand up to her. My confidence continued to grow until one day, brimming with anger, I stood up on the table and screamed, "I didn't cheat!" My classmates were in awe, and when word of what I had done went around, even other staff members started to like me.

I became aware that I was developing physically, and I took notice of the boys as they looked at me. Before I knew it, they were making me feel like a princess. Of course, jealousy was to be expected. Before I realized it, one girl in my class, Judi, had it in for me. When playing basketball, she started changing the rules of the game while we were playing, and so I took the basketball from her hands and kicked her and yelled at her while she was standing in front of me on the floor. All of the boys cheered and clapped for me. She ran to the washroom crying, and thereafter I was overwhelmed with boys asking me for a date. But I was still innocent at this time, despite my confidence.

Eventually Judi and I became friends. We once skipped class and stole a horse from a Bedouin's farm. I loved animals. Judi was scared of the horse, and so I handled it, and we ended up riding. I eventually took the horse to a sanctuary and left it there.

As I was gaining more and more confidence, I would tell my mother that I felt like a queen. She would say, "Yes, a queen but with a garbage mouth." I guess that was evidence of the harsh circumstances I was in.

As I grew into my early 20s, I was accepted into a Hebrew university in Jerusalem. I hated the system, and I wanted to go away. But I met one professor who saw me and asked me why I always had a long face. I told him I would be starting university soon, and he laughed. He said, "That's good." But I said that I wanted to study outside the country, in an English-speaking country. He mentioned a group that was meeting for vet university. I was shocked.

I went to register without telling anybody. After I'd confirmed the acceptance, I went home and told my parents, and they were also surprised. The following week, I left Jerusalem to go to Europe.

While in school, I also found a job in Germany. After I had graduated, I went to London, then Holland, and back to Germany again. I even got my externship to go to Prince Edward Island, Canada. I was on my own in the freezing cold weather on this island. There, I met a professor who asked me if I wanted to get into a PhD program. I immediately said yes. He said he would find funding for me.

I soon returned to Israel to work in a clinic and did not pursue the PhD. Meanwhile, I was telling everyone that I was going to get a PhD in Canada, but nobody believed me. Then, one day, I received a fax telling me that I had full funding and a salary for the PhD program.

I returned to Prince Edward Island, going through Toronto, when a lady in Toronto immigration customs stopped me from entering the country. (During my trip, I'd had this flashback of when I was 11 years old with the Yemenite teacher. I remembered she'd told me I will never get anywhere in life.) The immigration officer, told me told me she would make sure I will never do my PhD in Prince Edward Island. She took my passport and all of my papers. She locked me in a room. I had my period and couldn't change my pad. I knocked and banged on the door. Nothing. No food, no water, no wash room. The customs immigration officer manager told me I could not go to Prince Edward Island and would have to stay in Toronto. I would need to have my new documents made ready for the university at Prince Edward Island.

When I came back to reality after a 12-hour flight and with all my suitcases, I had missed my flight. After I was left waiting for three hours, the manager came and looked at me, shocked. I had missed my flight to Prince Edward Island and was losing my chance for student acceptance.

I had nobody in Canada, and so I called my mother. My family called a distant cousin who picked me up. I stayed in Toronto for eight weeks, but I still had to return to Prince Edward Island to begin my PhD. The university was waiting for me.

After eight weeks, I decided to hell with it. I am going to Prince Edward Island and going to school. Even though I wasn't supposed to, according to the customs immigration office manager, I went. So, here I was, an illegal student, and I couldn't register or get money or even use the computer at the university. This went on for three months. I rented a room from a lady, and I had to go to Buffalo, NY, a 13-hour drive only to the border, to obtain another student visa. With exams coming up, I couldn't make use of the library at the university. I was literally doing calculations by hand for my bio-physics class.

I was all by myself and freezing cold on Prince Edward Island. I took a taxi after the bus because public transportation wasn't very good. After several hours in a taxi at midnight, the taxi driver stopped and looked at me in a weird way. I grabbed my bag, opened the door, and ran. I was in the middle of nowhere, and then I realized that I was in St John, New Brunswick. It was pitch black and pouring rain. I ran as fast as I could because I was afraid. Finally, I saw an inn. They gave me a room, and the next morning I took a cab to the border to get my visa.

I was supposed to go to the Twin Towers area in New York City on September 11, 2011, to collect my papers, but I just decided to complete it in Buffalo. The other students could not believe how determined I was to be a PhD student. After I completed the papers I received from the school, I started my PhD. It wasn't easy at all. I chose to work with cloning, as I wanted to choose something that was not already studied a lot. My teachers were amazing; they were my mentors. They helped me, but most of the time I worked on my own initiative. I was determined to get good results.

Completing my PhD and finding work as a research scientist even before writing my CV was a big accomplishment. And before I knew it, after six months at work, I was promoted to clinical liaison manager and researcher. Despite the advancement, working for eight years also had its challenges, especially with life changes, such as getting married and having a baby while continuing to work. This was quite a balancing act. After another two years, I had my wonderful son, my second child, and was still working as a researcher.

Then came a major setback. I broke my leg when my son was only three months old. I had to have surgery and plates put in, but I still never stopped taking care of my kids while working simultaneously. Giving a bath to a two-year-old and a three-month-old baby has its difficulties, even more so with limited mobility.

As my children were growing up, I thought it was time for us to leave the beautiful island. I was helping my husband to find a job as an industrial research adviser in technology with the federal government at this time. In 2013, after 12 years of being on the island, we decided to move to Ontario, Greater Toronto Area. The move was not easy. I broke my leg again just before the move and was fitted with a cast up to my hip. I was still working as the lead scientist and head manager for the company that originally hired me. They did not want me to leave, and the CEO actually met with me in Toronto and offered me a higher position, but I accepted an offer from a bigger company.

After some time of working late hours, I found out a terrible thing was happening in my home. My husband—my rock and my strength, my supporter—was abusing our children. My little kids were being punched by him and were being verbally abused and humiliated. I guess everything happens for a reason, because the multinational corporation I was working for was bought out and we all were laid off. I thought, at least now I will be home looking for another job and I can protect my children.

While I was staying with my two little ones, they felt safe. My son, who had not spoken up until then, began to speak and was calmer and no longer afraid. He had been very nervous because of his father's abuse. The company that had purchased the previous one offered me a job that any other person would never refuse. But, because of the situation that was happening at home, I declined to accept the job as the director of the parasitology/immunology department in a huge company in North Carolina.

I was ashamed to call the police. I was ashamed to tell anyone that my husband of 14 years was an abuser. I wanted to keep my family together. But staying at home and not working was not an option. So, I decided to build my own company, VetInnovation, combining the latest, cutting-edge science with my passion for humans and animals, working with companies developing neurological and biotechnological products and redeveloping those products for the animal market.

As I was building my business and staying close to my little treasures, I was also working as a taxi driver, a coach, a teacher, a cook, but most of all a mom. It was not perfect, and God knows I am not a perfect mom, but I was there with my children while my husband was leaving for work at 10-11 a.m. and coming back at 4 a.m. the next morning. It felt like he didn't want to be at home with us. His explanation was that he had lots of work that could not be achieved from home. Obviously, I was ashamed of the situation, but I knew I had to build myself up so that I could build my company and show my kids that I could rise above the situation. And I wanted them to see me as being full of love and compassion for them and their dad, my husband.

Building the business and networking was a full-time job, as I was new in Ontario, and going to events and meeting entrepreneurs from various fields all over the world was a challenge. As I was building myself up, my husband started to become jealous. His parents, who were living with us at that time, were very influential, especially his mom, and she poisoned her son against me by saying that I was not good enough, that I was a parasite, was too fat for my dresses, and finally that I was actually going to the events and conferences to cheat on him! It was humiliating and shameful. I felt like a prisoner. But I was very determined to grow, to build my network, and to build my business.

As I travelled more, tensions were rising at home. I was traveling to conferences and leaving the little ones with him, hoping that he might change and all would be fine, but that was wishful thinking. It was stressful for the kids. They were crying constantly. Despite the fact that I cooked enough for them to be well fed every day and left the meals in the freezer for them, my kids were not fed. They were abused verbally and physically every day. So, when I returned home, they asked me not to travel without them, not to leave them alone with their father anymore.

During one of the conferences in India, I received an award for Iconic Woman of Leadership in Science. Despite that, my husband and his mother told me that I did not deserve anything and that my achievements meant nothing.

My decision to travel with my children for my business proved to be great for creating more opportunities in Europe and Israel. But coming back home was horrible. Documents from the house were gone. Money was gone. My husband took everything. And, as if he hadn't done enough already, he didn't want to leave the house, and he continued to punch the children again for no reason while they were playing a game. I asked him multiple times to leave. Feeling ashamed of this failure called marriage, feeling ashamed for my kids who were being punched and pinched by their dad, feeling ashamed by the name calling of me and my sweet children, I never called the police. I never told anybody until it was causing so much pain and stress for my precious treasures that I finally told my husband that we were getting a divorce and I wanted him out of my life.

He had caused so much damage, and he never wanted to get professional help. Nor did he ever want the kids to get professional help. Hearing them cry every day from fear, I had to take them to a psychologist in spite of his resistance. With so much commotion in our lives, being in hospitals, seeing doctors, and with all of the stress on me and my children, I was still trying to develop my business, determined for success, making every effort to be positive and to believe that we would overcome it all. I believed that this was just a bump in the road and we could thrive and be prosperous again. We would strive for peace in our home.

After time spent with lawyers, before the court, and with mediators, the judge said that no matter what the father had done, he should be in the kids' lives. I had no qualms with that in general, but when the father is abusive and he really doesn't care for his children and was never in their lives, it's different. From my point of view as a mother, this father needed to receive healing first, but nobody would listen to me or to my children. Nobody cared. My children were forced to meet with him and a mediator who was not qualified as a child psychologist and could not even see the children's stress. The mediator didn't see that it was not right to just push them towards their father to play with him when they didn't want to.

The whole experience was too much for them and they began throwing up next to the mediator, and nobody cared. The little kids were cleaning up the mess they'd made, which wasn't their fault, and their dad never even blinked when they were sick. When my daughter told the mediator she was scared and asked to not be forced to come and play like that, the mediator replied, "You must do it, so be quiet."

This experience has given me the strength to stick up for myself and fight the good fight for justice and to protect my children. Fighting for yourself and your darling ones while constantly thinking that you might lose your house and be outside, homeless, in spite of all of these achievements and all of the experiences in your career and in life makes you think. You never would believe this could happen to you, being pushed to the corner, thinking maybe you are a failure, wondering why and what are you fighting for anyway, feeling the shame of failure and the shame of losing everything you had, even going to the grocery store with declined debit and credit cards. I have been told by so many people, including family and people close to me, to give up the business, to forget about it, because it will never work and I will never succeed.

You may be wondering how all of this takes me back to the period of my childhood when I became so determined and promised I would not to forget my wishes or my beliefs, and when I realized my need to become a vet and a scientist. How does it bring me through the horror of the verbal abuse, the lack of confidence, the lack of self-belief? Quite simply: I don't want to give up. I've done it not only for my kids but for myself, so I could stop being ashamed.

Yes, maybe the marriage is over, but so is the disbelief in me and so is the abuse of my innocent children. I no longer see it as a failure. I don't see it as something to be ashamed of. I don't see it as my fault. I want to show my kids that when I look in the mirror I don't see regrets. I don't regret anything I've done. It has taught me who I am and what I am. I want to show my little ones that when I look in the mirror I see a strong, beautiful woman, successful but compassionate, honest and with integrity. I want to show them and myself that I am not ashamed because the woman I've become is enough. The woman I've become didn't lose herself in the process. She is strong and determined to succeed and to bring the latest cutting-edge innovation of science to humanity and for animals.

There will always be challenges in life. The funny part is, each challenge feels like a weight on your shoulders that you can't bear. Looking back, one might wonder how one got through the major changes that needed to happen. Whether it's to do with school or starting up a business, or those things combined with raising a family, the challenges are never ending. What I learned is that belief in myself, coupled with grit and determination, kept me sailing through without even knowing it.

Starting a business is generally hard, particularly in a saturated environment where demand isn't so high. On top of that, I've had the added difficulty of being surrounded by "friends" who give off negative vibes about my ambition. I have always said that fake friends are like shadows: they are there in brightness but fade away in dark times. But this should never be a deterrent. As much as it hurt, it made me stronger. Because I had an eye for my dream, nothing could phase me, no matter the odds. To make matters more complicated, there were setbacks, serious setbacks, such as being unwell. I had vertigo and migraines. There was no escaping it. It could strike at any time, and I never knew how long it would last. One would imagine that it would be impossible to carry on, especially with my condition. But I would always tell myself, don't be disheartened, this will pass, and I will be back in business, so to speak.

Just when you think things can't possibly get more complicated, they do. I had children, and things were never so rosy for them, either. It wasn't just a double whammy, not even a triple or quadruple whammy, but the whole shebang. I wouldn't wish what I went through on my worst enemy. But a part of me feels it was a blessing in disguise. Identifying my key strengths as though in an endurance test, working on my own initiative, and of course multitasking, there were several factors that kept me going.

One was my passion for animals, having advocated for them all my life, as well as my passion for science and innovation. I think that without any innovation, without science, without development, we cannot continue to evolve.

Changes in life will come. We, as human beings, will be able to survive on this planet because of new developments. People who were paralyzed can now walk. People who could not talk can now talk and converse. I'm not advocating for vaccinations and medications; I'm advocating for innovations, genetics, immunology, and biotechnology that is changing the world. Changing human and animal worlds. That's what keeps me going and keeps me determined to develop new ideas, develop new horizons for human kind and especially for animals.

Animals are being abused all over the world. We must teach people to be closer to animals and to understand this world better. That's what VetInnovation is about. That's why I'm so positive. I've had many negative people in my life, including in my family, people who were telling me to give up on my business. Toxic people can bring you down, but if you are passionate about what you do and truly love it, you'll be determined for success and prosperity, and you will win.

Doing it alone with no support, especially financially, isn't easy. But I am doing it. Most of all, I'm doing it for my children. Being a mother, I've had to be a role model for them, to demonstrate how to be strong in the face of adversity so that they would learn from and emulate me. I had to instill in them the mentality that nothing is impossible and giving up is not an option. I knew that I needed to love myself so that they would follow suit. Otherwise, how else would they learn? The onus was on me to illustrate this to them.

Guidance is key for children; they need a role model in life. I was that role model, and I still am. My children have been through so much, and I did my best to keep them in a stable environment and not to cancel their private schools or activities, even though it all cost thousands of dollars, all while building a business. At first the money wasn't flowing, but I was determined. That's why I'm so positive in bringing them up with the attitude that they are to never give up.

My parents and my brother were my anchors, but even they were negative at times and thought my business wouldn't work. Throughout the whole time, I never once feared failing. But a person is not an island. Having toxic people on one side can actually help one to be stronger, to believe more in oneself, to be tougher and finally to say no when it's time. On the other hand, people that are supporting and loving regardless of all of our faults, these people have been my rocks. These people are my strength. These people are making me proud of being in their circle and continuing with my passion, strengthening my calling to be an advocate for the ones that do not have voices, the ones that cannot talk back at all.

My life—my love for my beautiful, amazing children whom I am raising as the most important part of my life—is dedicated to showing them love and compassion but also power, determination, and independence. Being a mom, running a successful and prosperous business, and advocating for animals: these are what create my life's calling. This is my road to achievement.

Chapter 10
The Art Of Change
By Sharee Siva

A couple of years ago, I made a decision for myself to follow my heart and be true to myself. I wasn't sure what that even meant at the time, but I started listening and paying attention to my feelings of uneasiness and discontent. Slowly but surely my truth began to unfold and I chose to follow whatever it was saying. It certainly hasn't been easy at times - in fact it's been the most difficult period of my life, with lots of pain and sometimes a feeling of being quite selfish. Yet all those affected, including myself, have grown and transformed. Here I share with you what I have learned.

Dealing with Change

"Life is difficult."[2] The first sentence of a celebrated book, The Road Less Travelled, by M. Scott Peck, a clinical psychiatrist, sharing his wisdom, from the perspective of helping others in their very own personal journeys of spiritual growth. A fitting opening to a chapter focused on dealing with changes in one's life?

When I was first invited by John to contribute to this book I did not feel that I was emotionally ready to write about change. I felt like I was smack bang in the middle of it, still asking myself all of those seemingly unanswerable questions that arise during periods of pain or difficulty.

It took me many months to put pen to paper. I, myself, was going through an intense period of reflection, feeling stuck and confused as to where I was heading – a feeling that the ground beneath me had shifted,

---

[2] Peck, M. (2014). *The road less traveled.* 1st ed. New York: Touchstone.

and that one step forward was always followed by two steps back. I took many notes, and finally I could write this, no longer feeling immovable! Do I have the answers now? No, I don't. I have, however, learned that I possess great inner strength, courage, faith and wisdom. All of which serve for exciting possibilities to keep moving forward on my own personal journey of being true to who I am, and to go forth without attachment or expectation, to ultimately experience a true sense of personal freedom. For on the other side of fear is freedom!

"There is in the worst fortune the best chances for a happy change."[3]

Wake Up Calls

All of us, at some point in our lives, have or will, find ourselves facing the unexpected. Those curve balls in life, when we feel like we have been floored! Defining moments, realisations, obstacles or confronting events that occur, which leave us feeling as if the ground below has suddenly moved, that the path in which we thought we were on changes, that leaves us feeling confused, uncertain and questioning – a disconnection, "the gap between where we thought we'd be and where we actually are, between our expectations of what we hoped would happen and what has actually happened, between the life we planned and the life we inhabit."[4]

Perhaps a marriage partner has just announced that they want a divorce, a loved one or yourself becomes ill, a sudden death of a loved one, an accident or an injury, a financial crisis or an unexpected career change. Or, as in my instance, a moment of truth, a realisation that all I had been working towards no longer seemed important. My pursuit of financial security and success, left me feeling unfulfilled in the work that I was doing. An unfulfilling marriage and family life left me feeling empty and

---

[3] Euripides (Greek Philosopher (c. 480 – c. 406 BC). [online] Available at: http://belief net.com [Accessed 26 Apr. 2017].

[4] De Angelis, B. (2014). *How did I get here?*. 1st ed. [London]: Harper Element.

alone. It was as if all that I had strived for no longer seemed important to me. In hindsight, I see that it was not so sudden, it came with a process of decline and disillusionment. I had been living and continuing a way of life that didn't seem to fit anymore for some time. I was confused as to what my true values were and why had they changed. Ultimately having to face the truth, I found the courage to make the changes that I knew I needed to make – knowing very well that my choices would hurt others – and I was fearful of the fallout. The words of Alan Cohen capture the essence of this moment with eloquence and inspiration:

"The time comes when we can no longer find refuge in our defences. We discover, often with awe, that it is precisely our defences that have kept us in darkness! We tire of straining to protect ourselves, and we feel stifled and restricted by the walls we have built between our heart and others'. Our defences are not worth the love we lose in hiding. We cannot afford to maintain a citadel of fear at the cost of peace. In our efforts to keep pain away from our heart, we have also denied entry to joy. The moment arrives when we must break free and make a stand for who we are. That moment is now. The time has come to cast aside our cloaks of smallness and don the robes which honour our true magnitude. We must claim the strength to live in the dignity befitting our identity."[5]

Regardless of which side of change we find ourselves on, whether we ourselves are making the changes, or we are affected by unexpected change, sometimes seemingly brought about by others, we find ourselves in the same place. A transitional period, the time in between closing doors to the past and the requirement to undergo a personal transformation to redefine ourselves and our view of the future. Herein lies the profound gift to seek understanding of the present. If we recognise these moments as the greatest opportunities to learn, we can actively become participants in our own journey, releasing ourselves to live our own truths. "It is not how you deal with what is expected and hoped for in life that ultimately

---

[5] Cohen, A. (1994). *Dare to be yourself.* 1st ed. New York: Fawcett Columbine.

defines you and elevates you as a human being. Rather, it is how you interact with the unexpected, how you brave the unanticipated, how you navigate through the unforeseen and emerge, transformed and reborn, on the other side."[6]

My life has certainly not been immune to change, from both sides! From my own personal experience, and that I have witnessed in others' experiences, times of intense change tend to bring about the same conditions, feelings, and processes. One of the first conditions that arises is confusion. Sometimes the intensity of the confusion is so powerful that there is no other option but to find the strength and courage to question – or if to no avail – have blind faith that something greater than ourselves is operating for the best! Yet questions begin to, and continue to, intrude upon our consciousness; they appear to have no answers, but instead bring more questions! Once the process of questioning has begun, there is no turning back. To deny, defend or supress these questions is to rob ourselves of the opportunity to learn and grow. "If you get rid of the pain before you have answered its questions, you get rid of the self along with it."[7] Sincerely dwell on the questions themselves, with the knowledge that not all of the answers will come. In the words of Rainer Maria Rilke, an 18th century Austrian poet:

"...have patience with everything that remains unsolved in your heart. Try to love the questions themselves, like locked rooms and like books written in foreign language. Do not now look for the answers. They cannot be given to you because you could not live them. It is a question of experiencing everything. At present, you need to live the question. Perhaps you will gradually, without even noticing it, find yourself experiencing the answer, some distant day."

---

[6] De Angelis, B. (2014). *How did I get here?*. 1st ed. [London]: Harper Element.

[7] Carl Jung (Swiss Psychiatrist, 26 July 1875 – 6 June 1961),[online] Available at: http://belief net.com

Transitional periods can sometimes feel like we are lost. The 'maps' that we have built for ourselves, that have been guiding us thus far, no longer seem relevant or aren't working for us anymore. **Our very own personal maps perfectly reflect the individual reality that we inhabit.** To ignore the questions that arise from disillusionment is to ignore the opportunity to revise, or ultimately dispel our illusions and find truth. To live in the illusion is suffering and the cause for all our perceived problems. "The more effort we make to appreciate and perceive reality, the larger and more accurate our maps will be...the process of making revisions particularly major revisions is painful..." [8] Consequently, disillusionment presents an opportunity to end the illusion! It is an important distinction to make, that it is not you who is shattered, but your illusions!

"Disillusionment is the best thing that could happen to anyone. It means that something false has been undone, and the truth behind it is available to be discovered. The truth is always healing. Only illusions are painful. Therefore, be glad, even proud, that you have had the courage to learn a lesson that would break your illusions and replace them with greater strength and wisdom." [9]

Initially, it may be hard to swallow, although ultimately liberating – that the remaining answer, after endless questioning, lies in dispelling the illusion and finding the truth. If we ignore the truth, we will remain stuck, living in mediocrity disguised as comfort! Or even worse, we will reject new information as false and remain stuck in anger, blame, guilt, or unforgiveness. To live with truth or, in the words of Alan Cohen, "To dare to be yourself means to live in the spirit of power rather than weakness;

---

[8] Peck, M. (2014). *The road less traveled.* 1st ed. New York: Touchstone.

[9] Cohen, A. (1994). *Dare to be yourself.* 1st ed. New York: Fawcett Columbine.

to proceed from peace instead of clamouring to maintain defences; to want the reality of love more than the nightmare of fear."

"...the armour falls way to reveal the gold. A worthless image is crumbling, and the treasure is coming forth. It is the end of the cover up and the beginning of the radiance. In such a birth, there is great cause for joy."[10] The above passage gives reference to the true story of the Golden Buddha which now sits in a temple in Thailand, literally made of gold. "...a belligerent army...was on its way to invade the village. This disturbed the monks greatly, for they knew that if the army discovered the golden Buddha, it would be plundered and destroyed. Hastily the monks gathered...one monk offered a plan: Disguise the Buddha. 'Let us cover the Buddha with mud and stones and mortar...then the invaders will believe that the statue is merely a stone sculpture.' The idea met with unanimous approval, and the project was begun."[11] The army came and went and the Buddha remained in disguise long after the monks had passed, until one day many decades later the true state of the Buddha was revealed, and the Golden Buddha was restored to its original glory. We are all the golden Buddha, the mud, mortar, and stone being the illusions – our own personal fabrication to identify with our own self!

The Truth

Buddha, Zen master himself, offers profound insights to the nature of change. The Buddhist concept of impermanence is known as *annica*– an undeniable and inescapable truth of life, that nothing is fixed or permanent, and that everything is subject to change and alteration. Buddha illustrates the concept of impermanence by using the analogy of

---

[10] Cohen, A. (1994). *Dare to be yourself*. 1st ed. New York: Fawcett Columbine.

[11] Cohen, A. (1994). *Dare to be yourself*. 1st ed. New York: Fawcett Columbine.

a river. A river is a constant flow of successive moments, joining together to give the impression of one continuous flow. Our minds perceive this flow as one continuous reality. The Greek philosopher Heraclitus shared a similar analogy, "You can never step in the same river twice."[12] The suggestion is that all we know is the present moment; the previous moment cannot be repeated, just as the next moment is unknown. We are part of a constant cycle of flux. The universe never ceases in its workings. Life is a process and cycle of change – of birth, death, and regeneration, of exhaustion and renewal, of up and down. Everything is in a constant state of change, following the natural laws of the universe.

Therein lies the answer. **We must accept the reality of the present moment, for the present moment is the only truth or reality.** Ultimate truth is nirvana – and so, we find ourselves somewhere in between and we have begun the journey of understanding. Ignorance is not bliss: it is living your life in your manufactured illusions, which ultimately leads to more suffering. The opposite of ignorance is knowledge. "According to Buddha, the root problem is ignorance, which encourages attachments that lead to desires and cravings, which bring dissatisfaction and discontent. And, if ignorance is the problem, the solution must be knowledge. So, insight is redemption. Understanding is salvation."[13]

Change is life in motion. It's not a question of dealing with change; rather, it is a question of removing oneself, or remaining detached, from the effects, or the emotion of change. We are forced to find our own personal solution, the truth within, to seek an understanding of who we are, and our place in time.

---

[12] Heraclitus (Greek Philosopher c. 535 – c. 475 BC)),[online] Available at: http://belief net.com

[13] Foley, M. (2014). *The age of absurdity*. 1st ed. New York: Simon & Schuster UK

In order to better understand ourselves and to find our own personal truths, we have to look within. The first point of knowledge we have is that *we are*: the *I Am*. The next section gets a bit heavy, but I would like to share with you some of my own personal understanding.

"Your visions will become clear only when you can look into your own heart. Who looks outside dreams; who looks inside awakes." –Carl Jung

Understanding Consciousness

As there is no one universal definition of consciousness it is useful to study varying definitions and find the commonalities ourselves. It is up to us as individuals to reach a personal understanding of what consciousness means, and find its definitions in a language that is personally suitable. Developing an understanding of consciousness provides us with a foundation of truth to help us to find our own individual true natures and to grow and develop as individuals. In this section I will share with you my personal understanding, based on what I have read and experienced, from the premise that there is no one single answer.

"My life is a story of the self-realisation of the unconscious." –Carl Jung

Providing a definition for consciousness is a difficult task. Spiritual leaders, philosophers, and academics have sought to define what consciousness is since time immemorial. More recently, quantum physicists have entered the discussion. There are common themes amongst all viewpoints, although the terminology varies greatly. Most predominately is that consciousness is made up of both the "conscious mind" and the "unconscious mind." I hesitate to attach the word "mind," however, but do so for ease of understanding. It is a misconception that consciousness is limited to brain matter. Consciousness is not made up of matter; it is much subtler than that. Consciousness "perceives the world, remembers, thinks, compares, analyses, recognises, intellectualises and conceptualises the world through the brain. The brain is just the instrument."[14] "Mind is not located inside the brain. The brain is located inside the mind."[15] It's true. Read it again.

Consciousness is omnipresent. It does not live in the brain or the mind. The brain simply serves as the facilitator to life in action. The brain is simply an instrument, just like the heart or any other organ of our body, it is simply there to perform necessary bodily functions to keep us alive. We are much bigger than our brains. Engage your heart just as much as you engage your brain.

Buddha identified nine levels of consciousness which serves as a great foundation of understanding to begin from. The first five are the bodily senses of sight, hearing, touch, smell, and taste. Depending upon the sensory inputs, we experience differing levels of awareness. We can also practice to increase our awareness of the five senses, just as a person who becomes suddenly blind reports that the other four senses expand.

The sixth level is the mind. It is the analytical or linguistic mind that is capable of conceptualising, it "is the layer that integrates and processes the information from the various senses into a coherent whole (and)…corresponds closely with…the concept of mind…For most people, these first 6 levels of consciousness are where we spend most of our time in performing daily activities."[16] The seventh level is called *mano* or *manas* in *Sankrit*, and refers to our inner life. It can be described as that which knows oneself. "It is the number one discriminator whose

---

[14] Sabnis, S, Engineer & Yoga practitioner, (2016). Anon, (2017). [online] Available at: http://Brian Tracy blog

[15] Sabnis, S, Engineer & Yoga practitioner, (2016). Anon, (2017). [online] Available at: http://Brian Tracy blog

[16] Anon, (2017). [online] Available at: http://operation meditation blog [Accessed 26 Apr. 2017].

speciality is to say 'This is me. This is mine. This is not mine.' It creates belief in a self and distinguishes self from other."[17]

The eighth level is known as *alaya*, and in Buddhist terminology is "where karma resides," also known as the All Base or Storehouse consciousness. "A key feature of the *alaya* is that it stores seeds of delusion and habitual reactive tendencies, which can manifest dynamically in manas consciousness. The ninth level is that of pure consciousness, amala, enlightenment or Nirvana.

For the purpose of finding commonality in terminology, and therefore understanding, it is my view that levels six and seven (mind and identification with self) can roughly correlate to the "conscious mind" and eight and nine refer to the "unconscious mind." I like to think of the "conscious mind" as intellect, "the ability to acquire and apply knowledge and skills."[18] "It serves as 'linguistic consciousness'[19] with which we describe and think about the world." It gives name and form to things.[20] The "unconscious mind" I like to refer to as knowledge, – "awareness or familiarity gained by experience of a fact or situation."[21] It serves as '"unconscious awareness' that cannot be coded in language…sustained awareness rooted in the unconscious. We are fully aware of what is

---

[17] Thich Nhat Hanh (Buddhist monk) Goodreads. (2017). *Goodreads*. [online] Available at: http://GOODREADS.COM

[18] Murray, J., Bradley, H., Craigie, W. and Onions, C. (1961). *The Oxford English dictionary*. 1st ed. Oxford: Clarendon Press.

[19] Stanley, J., Loy, D. and Gyurme Dorje. (2009). *A Buddhist response to the climate emergency*. 1st ed. Boston: Wisdom Publications.

[20] Stanley, J., Loy, D. and Gyurme Dorje. (2009). *A Buddhist response to the climate emergency*. 1st ed. Boston: Wisdom Publications.

[21] Murray, J., Bradley, H., Craigie, W. and Onions, C. (1961). *The Oxford English dictionary*. 1st ed. Oxford: Clarendon Press.

happening, within and around us. Yet such experiences cannot be put into (or directed by) words."[22] The unconscious sees red; the conscious mind gives it the name "red."

Consciousness is infinite. The "conscious mind" has no limit as to what we can learn; yet it represents a miniscule part of consciousness. The "unconscious mind" represents that which precedes thought. It is infinite and omnipresent. The unconscious mind (awareness) performs all the functions to ensure survival without the requirement to access the conscious mind to apply thought. For example, we do not need to apply ourselves, or the action or direction of thought, in order to breathe, to digest food, to pump blood, to see, to feel, to taste, to smell, and so on. Unconscious awareness takes care of these functions in complete harmony, for most of the time! Moreover, we do not need to apply thought in order to feel or intuit the beauty of nature, music, art, humour, delight, and so on. Equally, we do not need to apply thought to feel such things as fear or pain. For example, if you touch something hot, you do not need to apply thought to realise that it is hot. Our conscious mind applies terminology to such experiences, but it does not need to be engaged to have the experience.

Both the unconscious and conscious are seemingly inextricably linked, and strive to keep a tight hold on one another. The "conscious mind," or intellect, serves to define the experience of the "unconscious mind" and, in doing so, engages the seventh level of consciousness which gives rise to our misconceived "ownership" of experience. It is in this misconception that the illusion of oneself manifests and masks one's true nature. Likewise, the "unconscious mind" acts as the storehouse of experience, a memory bank of everything that happens to you or that you perceive as to make happen. It stores snippets of imagery and

---

[22] Stanley, J., Loy, D. and Gyurme Dorje. (2009). *A Buddhist response to the climate emergency*. 1st ed. Boston: Wisdom Publications.

emotionalised thoughts, good and bad, which link together forming chains that that have no logical reasoning in their order, but are in some way connected to our deeper selves. Just like our dreams when we are asleep. Dreams themselves are born from the "unconscious mind" and serve to order life experience. However, I'm sure we could agree that dreams often do not have much logical order to them. L Ron Hubbard applies the name "engram" to these chains. Carl Jung and Dr DeMartini also speak of these chains and it is useful to research this further yourself.

The conscious mind allows these chains of irrational memory, stored in unconscious to intrude upon it, affecting and masking our perception of actual truth in ever present reality. Both are continually working together to ensure our survival, driven by fear and desire to avoid pain. It is here that we live in our comfort zones and limiting beliefs. It is here that attachment and expectation are created, which leads to suffering. By taking ownership of experience, we attach ourselves to expectations or outcomes of every action, which continues the circular motion of the illusion of self.

Quantum physicists' theory of the nature of consciousness helps to give form to the infinite nature and processes of consciousness in all its subtleties. This is potentially heavy, and so I'll try to keep it short. The first premise is that everything in the universe has both particle and wave nature, including ourselves! "Your idea of having a solid physical body is an illusion. Your body is made up of nothing but electromagnetically resonant waves."[23] "Consciousness is a non-material entity capable of independent, external existence, and not a property. Consciousness is not emergent [from the brain], and is eternal, similar to the electron. It can remain localised in the human brain and interact with the brain, and thereby, control the activities of the human body. While electrons in the brain behave as particles, these electrons prevent the consciousness from

---

[23] Dr John F Demartini. 2002 *The breakthrough experience*, Hay House, 1st Edition, United States

realising that it is part of a larger whole. When the electrons behave as a wave, the consciousness becomes aware of its existence outside the human mind."[24] Consciousness in the state of wave formation allows us to rationalise such phenomena as attraction, serendipity or synchronicity, auras, shared dreams, out of body experiences, premonitions, healing, and all manner of mystical occurrences.

I like the way Dr DeMartini describes the quantum physics of consciousness, and I take an excerpt from his book "The Breakthrough Experience:"

"Most of your body is empty space that contains minute fields of vibrating waves. You are a vibrating system. You have probably even said, 'I'm picking up strange vibes today,' or "Man, I don't like his vibes." You are made up of, pure vibrating light waves which physicists call quanta…A quantum light wave is composed of peaks and troughs, or positive and negative phases. Similarly, you are composed of peaks and troughs, or positive and negative emotions. The peak and trough phases correspond to the highs and lows of your consciousness; the same laws govern both. The positive phases of light waves are called positrons. The negative phases are called electrons. Neither of those phases by themselves is light; they are charged particles materialised in space and time. They each have mass, and participate in what is called density. If a complete light wave represented truth, then the positive or negative phases alone would represent only half-truths. When positive and negative phases join together in perfect balance, they birth light. Light doesn't move through space as a continuous bright streak; it pops in and out of existence as it jumps from one full wave, or quantum to the next. In between the points of light (photons) are the positive and negative

---

[24] END GAME TIMES. (2017). *THE AWAKENING – Quantum Mechanics of the Human Brain and Consciousness.* [online] Available at: https://endgametime.wordpress.com/the-awakening-quantum-mechanics-of-the-human-brain-and-consciousness/

half-quantum particles (positrons and electrons). That's what a quantum leap is: a jump from one radiant state of illumination to the next. Now you're probably wondering, 'Where is this guy going with all this physics stuff? Why is he talking about such abstract things?' I'm talking about your being, your physical nature as vibration. There are laws that govern those vibrations. When you apply those laws, you can understand what happens in life, and understanding is crucial to your illumination experience."

In reading the above excerpt one can liken the nature of quantum physics to Buddha's river.

A permanent state of non-localised consciousness is complete truth or enlightenment, which correlates the ninth level of pure consciousness, or Nirvana. The Buddhist concept of Nirvana originated from the Hindu concept of re-uniting with Brahman, both words are Sanskrit. Brahman can be described as "'the eternal, conscious, irreducible, infinite, omnipresent, spiritual source of the universe of finiteness and change.' Brahman is the source of all things and is in all things; it is the self or Atman of all living things."[25] It is also referred to as the Ultimate Reality. It is interesting that quantum physics of today is aligning with ancient spiritual teachings that date back to 2500 BC or earlier!

So how does this information help in one's quest for the truth? For a start, I think that there is a perception that we can either be enlightened individuals or not! It seems too hard, or unattainable, and so we tend to continue our life in the comfort or discomfort of our illusions. Having an increased understanding of consciousness provides us a with a point of knowledge to work from. It's as simple as changing the state of electromagnetic energy from particles into waves! But seriously, Buddha

---

[25] Anon, (2017). [online] Available at: http://religion facts

suggests that the progression is gradual, "Just as the ocean slopes gradually, with no sudden incline, so in the method training, discipline and practice take effect by slow degrees, with no sudden perception of ultimate truth."[26] The solution resides in liberating the "unconscious mind" from the "conscious mind." "Thich Nat Hanh describes this as follows: 'Manas consciousness loses its' grip on store consciousness, and the store consciousness becomes the Wisdom of the Great Mirror that reflects everything in the universe.'"[27]

How can we liberate the "unconscious mind" from the "conscious mind?" We have learned that sustained awareness, without the need to apply thought, stems from the "unconscious mind," and so this is where we should look for the truth. I like to think of the "unconscious mind" or storehouse consciousness, as a large circle of infinite space, with the interconnected chains of emotionalised images of the past floating inside. They take up a very small part of the surrounding infinite space. It is our task to operate from the blank space, thereby liberating our "conscious mind" from wanting to access these chains in its attempt for survival which is based on illusions. It is my view that if we can learn to engage the intellect of the "conscious mind" from the pure unconscious space we can observe and partake in life in motion from a point of truth.

Connecting with the pure unconscious bestows you access to extraordinary knowledge, energy, creativity, and genius that is beyond imagination. Pure consciousness is entire knowledge. "If you work long enough and hard enough to understand yourself, you will discover that this vast part of your mind [it is not of mind, however], of which you

---

[26] Buddha (as quoted in) Foley, M. (2014). *The age of absurdity*. 1st ed. New York: Simon & Schuster UK

[27] Stanley, J., Loy, D. and Gyurme Dorje. (2009). *A Buddhist response to the climate emergency*. 1st ed. Boston: Wisdom Publications.

now have little awareness, contains riches beyond imagination."[28] Or as quoted in the memoir of Carl Jung, 'Memories, Dreams, Reflections', Shen-hui states: "Those who see into the Unconscious have their senses cleansed of defilements, are moving toward Buddha-wisdom, are known to be with Reality, in the Middle Path, in the ultimate truth itself. Those who see into the Unconscious are furnished at one with merits as numerous as the sands of the Ganges. They are able create all kinds of things and embrace all things within themselves." [29]

What Does all this Mean?

How does this information help us to deal with difficult times in our lives? Firstly, if we know that change is paradoxically a permanent state, we can find comfort in that what we may be currently feeling will not be a permanent state. The choice is our own as to whether we remain stuck or choose to grow by seeking a deeper understanding of our own true nature. Secondly, every emotion has its equal and opposite emotion: on the other side of fear is freedom; on the other side of sadness is happiness; on the other side of right is wrong; and so on. It is entirely up to us as individuals to understand and fully embrace each part of our being to experience lightness, or as Dr Martini correctly calls love.

"There is no birth of consciousness without pain." –Carl Jung

We can begin to see that there is greater potential. There are skills that you can learn and master to navigate difficult times. Practising the art of focused attention to the very present moment is the first step. Focusing attention in the present suspends the usual executive functions of the

---

[28] Peck, M. (2014). *The road less traveled*. 1st ed. New York: Touchstone.

[29] Jung, C. (2013). *Memories, dreams, reflections*. 1st ed. [Place of publication not identified]: Stellar Books.

conscious mind so that the resources of the unconscious may unfold. In times of pain, it is useful to identify the very emotion that you are feeling. Naming the emotion, giving it form and shape, even creating a picture of it can help. Dwell intensely on it if you wish, and then let it go. It is not yours to own! "An emotion ceases to be a passion as soon as we form a clear idea of it."[30] Continual practice of applying focused attention on both the good and bad, will allow your truth to unfold, and you will learn to operate from the blank space. "Cognitively, mindfulness is aware that certain experiences are pleasant and some are unpleasant, but on an emotional level we simply don't react. We call this "equanimity" — stillness and balance of mind."

Also, go easy on yourself, and do not let past mistakes or the things that happen to you become you, because carrying and owning your emotions becomes heavy after a while. Remember, other than taking care of your responsibilities in a sensible fashion, you have no obligation to be or do anything for anyone but yourself.

Every experience, good and bad, is a gift. It's just a matter of opening it up to find what's inside!

Adversity does become our greatest teacher as it forces us to push through our comfort zones. "Your unconscious mind causes you to feel emotionally and physically uncomfortable whenever you attempt to do anything new or different, or to change any of your established patterns of behaviour."[31] We must teach ourselves to push through blockages or pain barriers. The technique of anchoring and focusing on the present can help us to do this. Next time you are feeling pain, anxiety, or fear, recognise that the "unconscious mind" and "conscious mind" are

---

[30] Spinoza (Dutch Philosopher 24 November 1632 – 21 February 1677), Foley, M. (2014). *The age of absurdity*. 1st ed. New York: Simon & Schuster UK

[31] Sabnis, S, Engineer & Yoga practitioner, (2016). Anon, (2017). [online] Available at: http://Brian Tracy blog

working together in the effort to protect you and your survival. Unless you are doing something inherently dangerous, you do not need protecting.

Push through the pain, intensely feel the emotion of it, yet do not get stuck in the emotion of it.

"Inspiration finds itself in action." –Picasso

Athletes often talk about being in flow or in the zone. It is an experience that is not limited to athletes, however, but is a relatable example. It comes from intense application to a task and pushing through the moments where you feel like giving up! It is exactly, at that moment, that applying focused attention works its magic! Give name and form to the present, and then return your focus to the end goal.

Being in flow is engaging with the present moment from the blank space. It is experiencing consciousness as omnipresent. It is where the electrons behave like waves. It is where consciousness becomes aware of its existence outside of the human mind. In flow, there is a loss of awareness to one's own self. It is an experience of being one with the universe, and the past and the future no longer exist. It is experience of the present moment in all its glory. It is living one's truth and is pure love! The fun part is that you can create whatever you want in here. Once you have felt it, even just for a moment, the truth, peace, and love seems boundless. It's freedom! Go with the flow. Create your own life. "May the force be with you!"[32]

---

[32] Star Wars, the movie, 1977 Lucasfilm Ltd, distributed by 20th Century Fox

About the Authors

1. **John Spender** - John started his first business at the age of 6 selling plaster of paris statues of Mickey Mouse and Donald Duck with his older brother. He later delivered pamphlets, papers, collecting trolleys, delivering milk and many other ventures all before he was 16. At 22 he had his own landscaping company completing council and government contracts, after giving up on that business due to an emotional break down.

   John learnt the value of a balance life, of investing in systems and the power of developing people to do the work for you, while they and the business grow together. He sold his last business for a healthy profit and began learning and studying about personal development and coaching with his journey taking him all around the world and learning many different modalities. That led John to transition into Coaching and Mentoring where he has now help over a thousands of people from around the world to live a life of freedom, fun and passion. He created the "A Journey Of Riches" book series and he is currently making a movie/doco about the gift in adversity.

   For more info visit www.ajourneyofriches.com

2. **Kay Newton** is originally from Yorkshire, England and renowned for her straight talking and wonderful listening skills. As a Midlife Stress Buster, Kay loves to unite and inspire people with her unique on-line 'Sensibly Selfish' style.

   Kay says; "I believe that in order to help yourself and those you love, you have to first put on your own oxygen mask, take in a huge breath of fresh air and exhale passion, purpose and authenticity. By doing so you can harness the power of stress."

After a thirty-year dream life in Mallorca, Spain, Kay and her husband of 25 years, have recently "Gone from an Empty Nest to 'No' nest in one step". They have, downsized, decluttered, sold the family home and moved to a two roomed, tin roofed home near a pristine beach, on the tropical island of Zanzibar, Tanzania, Africa.

"I have never been happier."

http://Kay-Newton.com

3. **Charlie Brown O'Shea** a 43 year old successful business man who is a co-owner & founder of Accme Coin Laundries, and has a successful and growing network marking business. Loving husband to his wife and business partner Efi and father of 3 beautiful children. He is a big believer in self help expanding mindset and helping others achieve greater good for themselves.

4. **Chris Drabenstott** - Truth seeker, thought leader, and bliss junkie, Chris is a dynamic nutrition & wellness entrepreneur, who left her career as a corporate technology executive to build the life of her dreams. Having tackled her own issues with severe obesity and alcoholism, Chris now thrives on teaching others the universal principles of how to release the emotional bonds of the past in order to activate the power of their fullest potential. She is also the founder of an online obesity support group called "LiveFULLy".

Chris is known for her unquenchable quest for knowledge of Divine wisdom and spiritual truth. Initially, this desire sprouted its roots through a calling into the ministry and admission to Baptist seminary, but it eventually sprung into full bloom with the discovery of personal development and a broadened acceptance of highly-varied spiritual practices.

"Avoid getting caught up in the illusion that this is the way it is" are her words to live by, which serve as a reminder to remain ever open to the infinite possibilities of new ideas, philosophies, and perspectives. Masterminding with accomplished scholars fuels Chris' deep purpose to cultivate creative outlets to teach self-healing and self-actualization. For more information contact Chris through her website: chrisdrabenstott.com.

5. **Theera Phetmalaigul**

www.theera.me

Email : theera@globalsuccesspartner.com

phetmalaigul@gmail.com

Before setting up Global Success Partner, Theera worked for almost 20 years with Esso Thailand, an Affiliate of major oil company ExxonMobil Corporation. He started as a Project Engineer and worked his way up the corporate ladder through various departments including Refining, Project Development, Supply&Logistics, until he became Regional Manager in Controller of ExxonMobil in Asia Pacific. He is a founder and President of Global Success Partner Company Limited, which providing business consulting for companies seeking business expansion into AEC (ASEAN Economic Community) markets, and specifically Cambodia, Laos, Myanmar and Vietnam. He also serves as a member in the Board of Directors of one of Thailand's Publically Listed Company.

Theera is a great example of someone in corporate world who would step outside his comfort zone and chasing his dream as entrepreneur and create business in many countries. What he discovered on his journey to riches while creating passive income from both business and investing as well as his ultimate dream to visit every country in the world will inspire you!

6. Born and raised in the Czech republic, **Pavel** is an entrepreneur and investor. He cares about sharing knowledge and democratizing technology- making it available to people and businesses that could not otherwise afford it. With his companies, Ecalypse.com and Rencato.com, he focuses on delivering more, happier customers to rental and tourism oriented businesses in more than 60 countries worldwide. Pavel earned his master's degree in Business valuation and administration at the University of Economics in Prague. After two and a half years in management consulting, he started Ecalypse as a company focused on providing booking systems to small and medium car rental companies. In 2016 Ecalypse launched Rencato, a platform which provides free technology to rental and tourism companies to reach more clients and provide them with better client experience. When not working, you will find Pavel doing sports, working on personal development or traveling.

7. "**Karen Higginbottom**: Grew up in the English countryside in the county of Derbyshire in the UK. After leaving home at the age of 18 to go to university in Leicester, she spent time studying and working in Cambridge before moving to London to pursue a PhD in cancer research. A life changing health challenge led Karen to question many aspects of her life, and to the realization of the deep need to be true to her-self. Karen now lives in the US and enjoys leading a more authentic life where she enjoys connecting with people and challenging them to uncover their own truths.

    To learn more go to www.karenhigginbottom.com"

8. **Isabella Verzberger's** journey edging to a rise to prominence can be put down to a combination of grit, determination, well organized, and deadline oriented. She Completed her DVM, she worked in a small animal hospital, in Israel, Germany and Netherlands and is now currently residing in Canada. In 2002 She started a PhD in Canada

and finished 2007, she worked in pharmaceuticals and neutracuetical companies, developing products for animals. She got married, had to go through painful fertility procedures for 6 years to have her children, to find out that her husband becoming an abuser towards the kids. In 2015 Isabella had opened her new company, Vetinnovation Inc. which bridges between Human and Veterinary medicine. Developing products, diagnostic devices for animals. In 2016 she decided to leave her husband, following 14 years of marriage while her kids are still very young. AS it is not easy to be a single mom still fighting her ex that denies all kind of abuse towards her but especially the kids. As her ex-husband and even authorities like a judge telling her to close the business and go back to work corporate, maybe making more money. Isabella is determined to have her business, so she can thrive for success, passion for animals and people and help humanity and animals to evolve for better healthier life, but most of all spending time with her amazing kids Lana and Ethan, to protect them and teach them no fear but love and compassion.

9. **Sharee Siva** is a self described theorist, who is deeply curious as to the paradoxical nature of what it means to be human!

She is an abstract painter, collage artist and sculptor. Her works explore abstract concepts such as 'patterns' of consciousness', 'impermanence', 'reflection', and 'language and its historical and cultural significance'. Her work is often quirky in nature, connecting the everyday with the esoteric.

Writing is a recent addition to her creative passions, and begins with the intention of making a positive difference to the life of others. Her writing stems from the foundation of living from ones own personal truth, sharing her theories on topics such as love, relationships, adversity, purpose, consciousness, spirituality, and other aspects of life in action.

Sharee was born in, and resides in Melbourne with her two daughters. Upon completion of her VCE, Share was awarded a scholarship to study a Bachelor of Business Systems at Monash University, Clayton. She then began a business career, firstly with IBM Global Services and moved on to be a founding member of Omnivision Pty Ltd. She still plays a small role in this company, however prefers to spend her time following her creative passions.

www.ingramcontent.com/pod-product-compliance
Lightning Source LLC
Chambersburg PA
CBHW060531100426
42743CB00009B/1491